HMH SCIENCE DIMENSIONS™

Grade 2

This Write-In Book belongs to

Karh

Teacher/Room

Houghton Mifflin Harcourt™

Consulting Authors

Michael A. DiSpezio
Global Educator
North Falmouth, Massachusetts

Marjorie Frank
Science Writer and Content-Area
  Reading Specialist
Brooklyn, New York

Michael R. Heithaus, PhD
Dean, College of Arts, Sciences & Education
Professor, Department of Biological Sciences
Florida International University
Miami, Florida

Cary Sneider, PhD
Associate Research Professor
Portland State University
Portland, Oregon

Front cover: sand castle ©koya79/Dreamstime

Back cover: sand castle ©koya79/Dreamstime

Program Advisors

Paul D. Asimow, PhD
Eleanor and John R. McMillan Professor of Geology and Geochemistry
California Institute of Technology
Pasadena, California

Eileen Cashman, PhD
Professor
Humboldt State University
Arcata, California

Mark B. Moldwin, PhD
Professor of Space Sciences and Engineering
University of Michigan
Ann Arbor, Michigan

Kelly Y. Neiles, PhD
Assistant Professor of Chemistry
St. Mary's College of Maryland
St. Mary's City, Maryland

Sten Odenwald, PhD
Astronomer
NASA Goddard Spaceflight Center
Greenbelt, Maryland

Bruce W. Schafer
Director of K-12 STEM Collaborations, retired
Oregon University System
Portland, Oregon

Barry A. Van Deman
President and CEO
Museum of Life and Science
Durham, North Carolina

Kim Withers, PhD
Assistant Professor
Texas A&M University-Corpus Christi
Corpus Christi, Texas

Adam D. Woods, PhD
Professor
California State University, Fullerton
Fullerton, California

Classroom Reviewers

Michelle Barnett
Lichen K-8 School
Citrus Heights, California

Brandi Bazarnik
Skycrest Elementary
Citrus Heights, California

Kristin Wojes-Broetzmann
Saint Anthony Parish School
Menomonee Falls, Wisconsin

Andrea Brown
District Science and STEAM Curriculum TOSA
Hacienda La Puente Unified School District
Hacienda Heights, California

Denice Gayner
Earl LeGette Elementary
Fair Oaks, California

Emily Giles
Elementary Curriculum Consultant
Kenton County School District
Ft. Wright, Kentucky

Crystal Hintzman
Director of Curriculum, Instruction and Assessment
School District of Superior
Superior, Wisconsin

Roya Hosseini
Junction Avenue K-8 School
Livermore, California

Cynthia Alexander Kirk
Classroom Teacher, Learning Specialist
West Creek Academy
Valencia, California

Marie LaCross
Fair Oaks Ranch Community School
Santa Clarita, California

Emily Miller
Science Specialist
Madison Metropolitan School District
Madison, Wisconsin

Monica Murray, EdD
Principal
Bassett Unified School District
La Puente, California

Wendy Savaske
Director of Instructional Services
School District of Holmen
Holmen, Wisconsin

Tina Topoleski
District Science Supervisor
Jackson School District
Jackson, New Jersey

You are a scientist.
You are naturally curious.

You may have wondered things such as these.

Why does ice melt?

Why does your heart beat?

Where does thunder come from?

What do animals need to grow?

HMH SCIENCE DIMENSIONS™

will SPARK your curiosity.

Where do you see yourself when you grow up?

Draw what you want to do when you grow up.

Be a scientist.
Work like real scientists work.

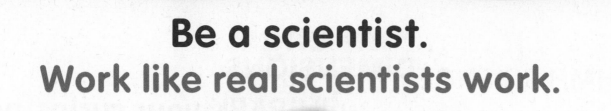

Solve problems.

Have fun.

Explain why.

Be an engineer.
Solve problems like engineers do.

Design.

Solve.

Test.

Explain your world.
Start by asking questions.

Do.

Think.

Share.

There is more than one way to the answer. What is yours?

Work in teams.

Make a claim.

Support with evidence.

© Houghton Mifflin Harcourt

© Houghton Mifflin Harcourt

Life Science

Unit 3 • Environments for Living Things 107

Earth and Space Sciences
Unit 4 • Earth's Surface............................ 183

Unit 5 • Changes to Earth's Surface 221

© Houghton Mifflin Harcourt

Safety in Science

Doing science is fun. But a science lab can be dangerous. Know the safety rules and listen to your teacher.

- ⊘ **Do not eat or drink anything.**
- ⊘ **Do not touch sharp things.**
- ✓ **Wash your hands.**
- ✓ **Wear goggles to keep your eyes safe.**
- ✓ **Be neat and clean up spills.**
- ✓ **Tell your teacher if something breaks.**
- ✓ **Show good behavior.**

Safety in Science

Circle the pictures where a safety rule is being followed. Place an X on the pictures where a safety rule is not being followed.

Unit 1
Engineering Design Process

Unit Project • Runaway Wagon

How can you stop a wagon from rolling away when you let go of its handle? Investigate to find out.

Unit 1 At a Glance

Unit Vocabulary

engineer a person who uses math and science to define and solve problems (p. 6)

design process a set of steps that helps an engineer define a problem and plan, test and share a solution (p. 6)

solution an answer to a problem (p. 6)

strength a good feature (p. 24)

weakness a flawed feature (p. 24)

Vocabulary Game • Guess the Word

Materials
• 1 set of word cards

How to Play
1. Work with a partner to make word cards.
2. Place the cards face down in a pile.
3. One player picks the top card but does not show it.
4. The other player asks questions to guess the word.
5. When the word is guessed correctly, the other player takes a card.

Children used a design process to put together these robots.

By the End of This Lesson

I will use the steps of a design process to define and solve a problem.

Ramps

Explore online. ▶

Look at the pictures to explore
how people use ramps.

A ramp is a flat surface with one end higher than
the other. People use ramps to solve problems.

Can You Solve It?

✏️ How can a ramp solve a problem?

_____

_____

_____

What Engineers Do

Explore online. ▶

Explore the steps of a design process that an engineer follows.

1. Define a Problem
2. Plan and Build
3. Test and Improve
4. Redesign
5. Communicate

An **engineer** uses math and science to define and solve problems, such as how to get to the top of a tall building or how to cross a river. Engineers may solve different problems, but they always use a similar set of steps, called a design process. A **design process** helps engineers define a problem and plan, test, and share a solution with others. A **solution** is an answer to a problem.

✏️ **What does an engineer do?**

_____

_____

Step 1–Define a Problem

Explore online. ▶

Look at the picture to explore how to define a problem.

Emma observes her dad trying to put a box into his car. The box is too heavy for him to lift. Emma thinks this is a problem that needs a solution. She has defined a problem, which is the first step of a design process.

✏️ **What is the first step of a design process?**

_____

_____

✋ **Apply What You Know**

Evidence Notebook • Work with a partner to define a problem within your classroom. Record it in your Evidence Notebook.

💡 **Asking Questions and Defining Problems** Go to the online handbook for tips.

Step 2—Plan and Build

Explore online.

Look at the picture to explore how to plan and build a design solution.

How does Emma help her dad with the problem with the box? She knows a ramp can help move objects. Emma makes a plan. She draws a model to show how the ramp will work. Then she builds her model using paper. Emma has done the second step of a design process—plan and build.

✏️ **What takes place in Step 2 of a design process?**

_____

_____

🖐️ Apply What You Know

Evidence Notebook • Think back to the classroom problem you defined. Work with a small group to plan and build a solution. Record your plan in your Evidence Notebook.

Developing and Using Models Go to the online handbook for tips.

Hands-On Activity

Engineer It • Build a Better Lunchbox

Materials
_____

_____

Ask a Question

_____

Test and Record Data **Explore online.** ▶

Step **1** Define a Problem

 What is wrong with the lunchbox? Which materials could help you solve the problem? Record your observations.

Lunchbox	Materials

Step **2** Plan

Plan a solution. Draw and add labels.

Step 3 Build

Follow your plan. Use your materials.
Build your solution.

Step 4

Share your solution with a partner. Compare
your design solutions. How does each one
solve the problem? Record your ideas.

Your Solution	Both	Your Partner's Solution

Make a claim that answers your question.

_____

_____

_____

What is your evidence?

_____

_____

_____

Step 3—Test and Improve

Explore online.

Look at the pictures to explore how to test and improve a design solution.

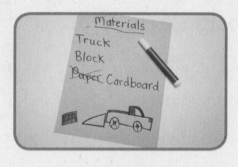

Will Emma be able to solve the problem? She tests her ramp to see if the block gets in the truck. The ramp is not strong or stable enough to support it. How can Emma improve it? She uses more stable materials to rebuild. She has done the third step of a design process—test and improve.

What is the next step after plan and build?

_____.

Apply What You Know

Evidence Notebook • Test and improve your solution to the classroom problem. Use your observations as evidence and record them in your Evidence Notebook.

Step 4—Redesign

Explore online.

Look at the picture to explore how to redesign a solution.

Emma improves her ramp by redesigning it. She uses cardboard, which is stronger and more stable. She tests the new ramp. It works on the first try! Sometimes engineers must redesign a solution more than once until it works. Emma has done the fourth step of a design process.

What happens during Step 4 of a design process?

_____

_____

Apply What You Know

Evidence Notebook • Did your solution work? Can you improve it? Redesign your solution. Use your observations as evidence and record them in your Evidence Notebook.

Step 5—Communicate

Explore online.

Look at the picture to explore how to communicate about a design solution.

Emma found a design that works. How does Emma communicate, or share, what she did with others? First, she photographs the ramp. Then, she describes the ramp, the materials she used, and how she designed it. Emma has completed the last step of a design process.

✎ **What are some ways to communicate the results of a design process?**

Apply What You Know

Evidence Notebook • Communicate your results. Write a summary of how you solved a problem in your classroom by following a design process. Use evidence to support your summary. Compare your solutions with your classmates'.

© Houghton Mifflin Harcourt

Take It Further
Engineer It • Make Your Lunchbox Better

Explore online.

Step ① Test and Improve

Test your solution. Record the results. Identify ways to improve your design.

_____

_____

Step ② Redesign

Define a different way to solve the problem. How does its structure relate to its function?

Step ③ Communicate

Do the Math! • Complete a bar graph to show the materials that you and your classmates used.

Ways to Make a Better Lunchbox

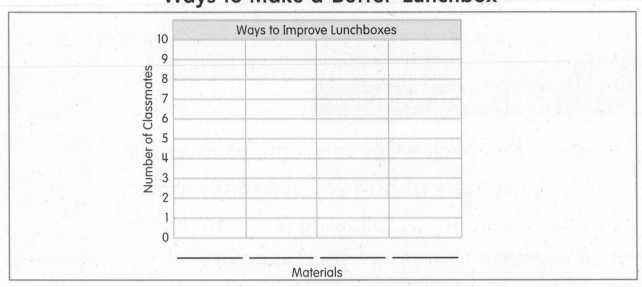

Take It Further

Careers in Science & Engineering • Mechanical Engineer

Explore more online.
- Engineer It • Make Your Lunchbox Better

Explore online. ▶

Mechanical engineers invent machines and make them work better. They use a design process to do their jobs.

Some mechanical engineers look for ways to improve machines so they are easier to use.

One engineer uses a computer to plan and build a model. Another engineer tests the model to see how it works.

Read, Write, Share!

Find out more about mechanical engineers. Ask questions, such as:

- What do they do?
- Where do they work?
- How do they work?

Do research to answer your questions.

Draw or write to record your answers.

Name _____

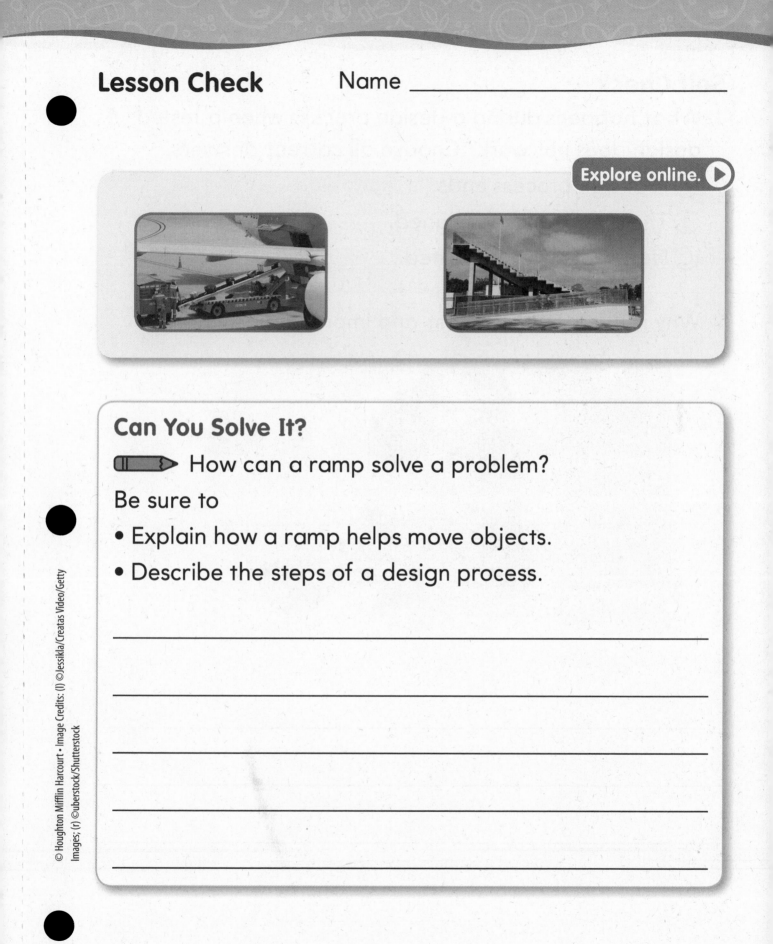

Explore online. ▶

Can You Solve It?

▭▬▷ How can a ramp solve a problem?

Be sure to

• Explain how a ramp helps move objects.

• Describe the steps of a design process.

_____

_____

_____

_____

_____

Self Check

1. What happens during a design process when a tested design does not work? Choose all correct answers.

Ⓐ A design process ends.

Ⓑ The old plan is redesigned.

Ⓒ New redesigns are tested.

2. Why is it important to test and improve a design?

_____

_____

_____

3. Which step of a design process is the girl doing?

(A) Define a Problem

(B) Plan and Build

(C) Test and Improve

4. Sam makes a ramp. He puts toy cars on it, but the ramp does not work well. What is Sam's next step?

(A) Plan and Build

(B) Test and Improve

(C) Redesign

5. Which step of a design process are the children doing?

(A) Define a Problem

(B) Plan and Build

(C) Test and Improve

Different solutions can solve the same problem.

By the End of This Lesson

I will be able to compare the strengths and weaknesses of different design solutions.

© Houghton Mifflin Harcourt • Image Credits: ©Sean Pavone/iStock/Getty Images Plus/Getty Images

How We Use a Design Process Every Day

Explore online. ▶

Look at the picture to explore the stop sign design.

The stop sign is made of strong metal, but its solid design twists in the wind. What are the weaknesses in its design? What changes to its structure could make the stop sign design stronger?

Can You Solve It?

 Identify strengths and weaknesses in the stop sign's design. What are two ways to make it better?

_____

_____

One Problem, Many Solutions

Explore online. ▶

Look at the pictures to explore how Diego plans and builds solutions to improve his backpack.

Most problems have many solutions. Diego has defined a problem with his backpack. Its thin straps hurt his shoulders. Diego comes up with several solutions.

One solution uses bandages. A second uses bubble wrap. A third uses a pool noodle, and the fourth uses a paper towel roll. Diego tests all to see which one works best.

Apply What You Know

✏️ Work with a partner to design two more solutions to Diego's backpack problem. Test your solutions. Record the results. Then compare the results to decide which solution is better.

Analyzing and Interpreting Data Go to the online handbook for tips.

22

Do the Math!

Diego's classmates tested his backpack solutions. Then they took a class poll to find out which solution each child thought worked the best.

Make a Bar Graph
Go to the online handbook for tips.

Explore online.

Which solution was most comfortable?

- Six children liked the bandages best.
- Ten children liked the bubble wrap best.
- Four children liked the pool noodle best.
- One child liked the paper towel roll best.

✏️ **Use this data to draw bars in the graph.**

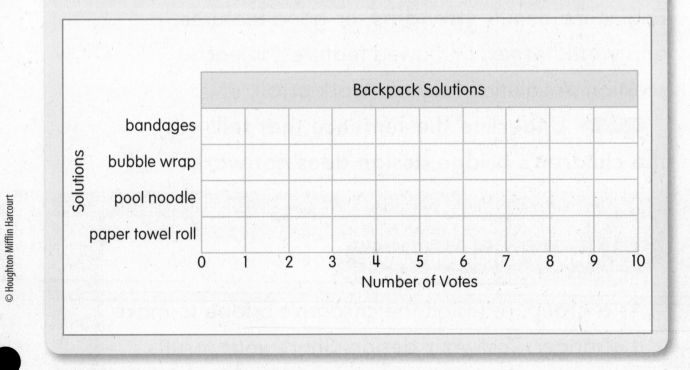

Backpack Solutions

Solutions: bandages, bubble wrap, pool noodle, paper towel roll

Number of Votes: 0 1 2 3 4 5 6 7 8 9 10

Lesson 2 • Engineer It • How Can We Compare Design Solutions?

23

Build and Test a Solution

Explore online. ▶

Look at the pictures to explore how children use books and paper to build a bridge design.

The children test a bridge design. They observe the flat paper is too weak and thin to hold the pencil.

Engineers plan and build many possible solutions. They test each one to see how well it works and to find ways to improve it. Engineers identify **strengths**, or good features, and **weaknesses**, or flawed features, in each solution. A solution may not work at all.

✏️▷ **Underline the sentence that tells why the children's bridge design does not work.**

🖐️ **Apply What You Know**

As a group, redesign the children's bridge to make it stronger. Test your design. Share your results with your class.

Compare Design Solutions

Explore online. ▶

Look at the pictures to explore how children improve their bridge design.

The first bridge design did not work because the structure of the flat paper is too weak and too thin to support the pencil. The children fold the paper like a fan and test their new design to see if it works better. They observe the folded paper is stronger and does not bend easily. This new design can support many pencils.

Why does the folded paper design work better? Choose all correct answers.

Ⓐ It is taller

Ⓑ It is stronger.

Ⓒ It does not bend easily.

Lesson 2 • Engineer It • How Can We Compare Design Solutions?

25

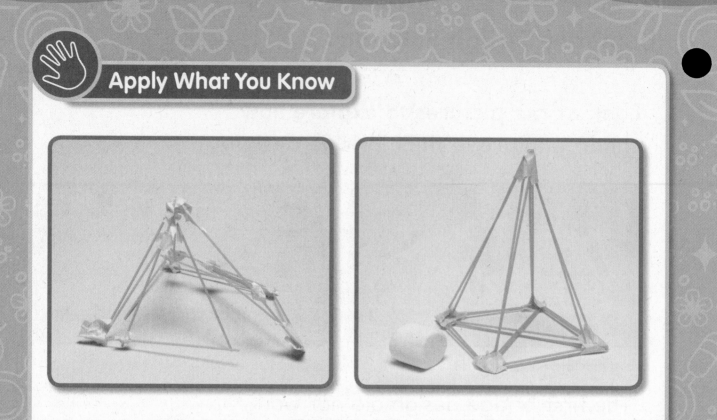

Read, Write, Share! • **Evidence Notebook** After you complete the Hands-On Activity, return to this page. Work with a partner to compare the shape and the structure of the two towers. Do you observe any weaknesses in either tower? Which tower has a better design? Use evidence to support your answer. Record it in your Evidence Notebook.

Structure and Function • Recall Information
Go to the online handbook for tips.

Name _____

Hands-On Activity

Engineer It • Compare Strengths and Weaknesses of Design Solutions

Materials

_____

_____

Ask a Question

_____

Test and Record Data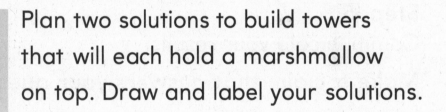

Step 1

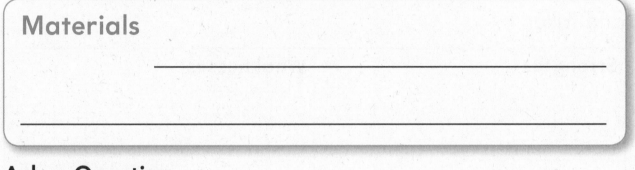

Plan two solutions to build towers that will each hold a marshmallow on top. Draw and label your solutions.

Step 2

Use the materials. Follow your plan. Build your solutions.

Step 3

Test your design solutions. Place a marshmallow on the top of each one.

© Houghton Mifflin Harcourt

Step 4

Compare your test results. Identify strengths and weaknesses of each design. Make changes to your designs to make the towers stronger and taller.

Strengths	Weaknesses

Step 5

Communicate your results.

Make a claim that answers your question.

_____

_____

_____

What is your evidence?

_____

_____

Take It Further

People in Science & Engineering •
Gustave Eiffel

Explore more online.

• Blast to the Past

Explore online. ▶

Gustave Eiffel was a structural engineer. He designed bridges and other structures made of metal. He studied how air moved around things. He used what he found out to build structures that could stand up to strong winds.

Eiffel designed the Eiffel Tower in Paris, France. The tower was built in 1889. It was 986 feet tall. For many years, it was the tallest building in the world. How could such a tall building resist high winds? Eiffel designed the tower to solve this problem.

Lesson 2 • Engineer It • How Can We Compare Design Solutions?

29

How did Eiffel design the tower to resist high winds? First, he used a special kind of iron to make the tower strong. Then, he built two kinds of bases to set it firmly in the ground.

Eiffel designed a curved frame so wind could move around it. Then he had workers heat the metal pins that held pieces together. When the pins cooled, they shrank to a tight fit. All these ideas made the tower strong.

How did Gustave Eiffel design the Eiffel Tower to resist high winds? Choose all correct answers.

Ⓐ He used a special, stronger kind of iron.

Ⓑ He included curves in the metal design.

Ⓒ He set the tower on two kinds of bases.

Lesson Check

Name _____

Explore online.

Can You Solve It?

 Identify strengths and weaknesses in the stop sign's design. What are two ways to make it better? Be sure to

- Identify weaknesses in the stop sign's design.
- Describe two solutions that will make the design stronger.

_____

_____

_____

_____

Self Check

1. Which **best** describes the step in a design process that the children are doing?

Ⓐ Test and Improve

Ⓑ Redesign

Ⓒ Communicate

2. What does an engineer do when a design solution does not work? Choose all correct answers.

Ⓐ make changes

Ⓑ define a new problem

Ⓒ test new designs

3. Alma builds two bridge models. Then she tests them. What tells her how well each model works? Choose the **best** answer.

Ⓐ questions

Ⓑ data

Ⓒ designs

4. Tariq tested three paper airplane models. The bar graph shows how far each model flew. Which model worked **best**?

 Ⓐ Cobra

 Ⓑ Dart

 Ⓒ Shadow

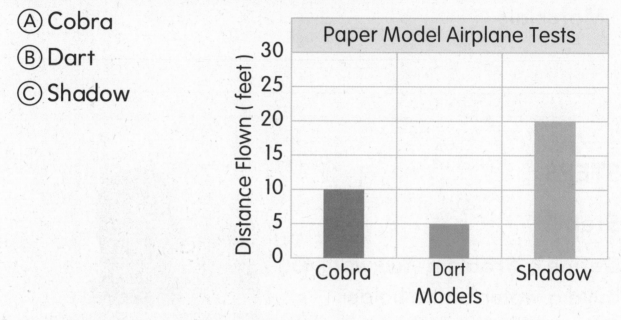

5. This door will not stay closed. Why is it important to find more than one solution to this problem?

 Ⓐ The first solution never works, so other ideas are needed.

 Ⓑ Developing more than one solution helps to find the best one.

 Ⓒ Working on several designs gives time for the door to fix itself.

Materials

_____

_____

STEPS

Step 1

Define a Problem You want to build a water bottle holder that will keep your hands free but your water bottle nearby.

Step 2

Plan and Build Plan at least two solutions. Think about the materials you will need and then build your solutions.

Step 3

Test and Improve Test your designs. Which one works better? How can you improve that design?

Step 4

Redesign Change the materials, or change how you put the materials together to make the water bottle holder better.

Step 5

Communicate Share your solution. Explain which materials make up your water bottle holder and why you chose to use them. Use evidence to tell how your design solves the problem.

✔ Check

_____ I built a water bottle holder that keeps my hands free but my water nearby.

_____ I tested my water bottle holder.

_____ I redesigned my water bottle holder to make it work better.

_____ I used evidence to show how my solution solved the problem.

_____ I shared my design with others.

Name _____

1. Which is **true** about engineers? Choose all correct answers.
   Ⓐ They use science and math to solve problems.
   Ⓑ They design solutions that cause problems.
   Ⓒ They use a design process to solve problems.

2. Carlo tests model cars he built for a race. What helps him decide which car to choose for the race? Choose the **best** answer.
   Ⓐ color
   Ⓑ data
   Ⓒ questions

3. The bar graph shows results from the three cars Carlo tested. Which model car traveled farthest?

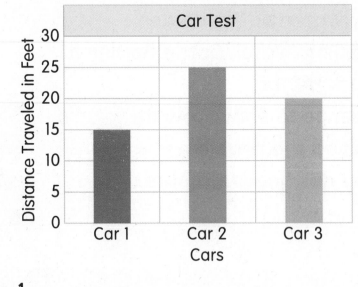

   Ⓐ Car 1
   Ⓑ Car 2
   Ⓒ Car 3

4. This boy is having trouble riding his bike. Which step of a design process does this picture show?

   Ⓐ Define a Problem

   Ⓑ Plan and Build

   Ⓒ Test and Improve

5. Arum sees a boy with his pant leg caught on a bike chain. She plans and builds a design solution to solve this problem. What will she do next?

   Ⓐ Redesign

   Ⓑ Test and Improve

   Ⓒ Communicate

6. Josie has redesigned and tested her model. The new model solves her problem. What should she do next?

   Ⓐ communicate her results

   Ⓑ find a new problem

   Ⓒ redesign again

7. What is the design weakness in this shopping bag?

Ⓐ its sides

Ⓑ its handles

Ⓒ its bottom

8. Yolanda wants to keep the sun off her face. Which hat should she choose for its design strength?

 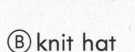 

Ⓐ sun hat Ⓑ knit hat Ⓒ narrow brim hat

9. What should you do if your design solution does not work? Choose all correct answers.

Ⓐ test new designs

Ⓑ test the design until it works

Ⓒ make changes to improve the design

10. Aaron built a launcher. Which step of a design process is he doing now?

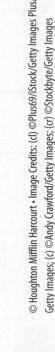

Ⓐ Redesign

Ⓑ Test and Improve

Ⓒ Plan and Build

Unit 2
Matter

Unit Project • Explore Melting

What is the fastest way to change ice to water? Investigate to find out.

Unit 2 At a Glance

© Houghton Mifflin Harcourt • Image Credits: ©Preartiq/Shutterstock

Unit Vocabulary

matter anything that takes up space (p. 44)

property one part of what something is like (p. 45)

solid a state of matter that keeps its shape (p. 48)

liquid a state of matter that takes the shape of its container (p. 49)

melt a change when a solid becomes a liquid (p.74)

freeze a change when a liquid becomes a solid (p. 80)

reversible a change that can be undone (p. 90)

irreversible a change that cannot be undone (p. 93)

Vocabulary Game • Make a Match

Materials
- 1 set of word cards
- 1 set of definition cards

How to Play
1. Work with your partner to make word and definition cards.
2. Place the cards face up on a table.
3. Take turns picking a word card, reading the word, and matching it to a definition.
4. If you make a match, keep the cards.
5. If there is no match, put the cards back.

These balls have different properties.

By the End of This Lesson

I will describe and classify materials by their properties. I will choose the best materials to fit my purpose.

Materials Are Different

Think about how bike tires are used. Why are bike tires made of rubber? What makes this material different from other materials?

Explore online. ▶

Can You Explain It?

What is another use for rubber?

_____

_____

_____

Properties of Matter

Matter is anything that takes up space. Look at the pictures to explore some properties of matter.

Explore online. ▶

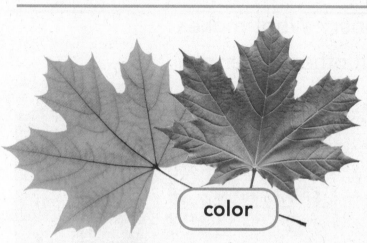

color

Color is a property you can see. One leaf is green. The other leaf is red.

shape

Shape is the form a material has. It is a property you can see. The safety object is shaped like a cone. The box is shaped like a rectangular prism.

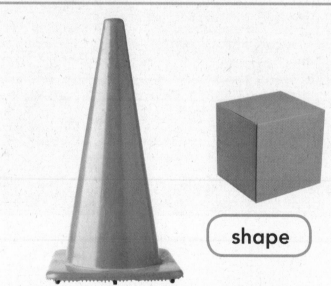

hardness

Hardness is how easy it is to change the shape of a material. It is a property you can feel. A marble is hard. A cotton ball is soft.

Texture is what a material feels like. It is a property you can feel. The light brown rock is rough. The dark brown rock is smooth.

texture

Flexibility is how much a material can bend. It is easy to bend the chenille sticks. They are flexible. It is not easy to bend the craft sticks. They are stiff.

flexibility

Matter has properties. A **property** is one part of what something is like. You can observe properties of matter with all your senses.

Color, shape, hardness, and flexibility are some properties of matter. These properties can be used over and over to describe matter. This forms a pattern.

Patterns
Go to the online handbook for tips.

Write words in the chart below to identify the properties of each object.

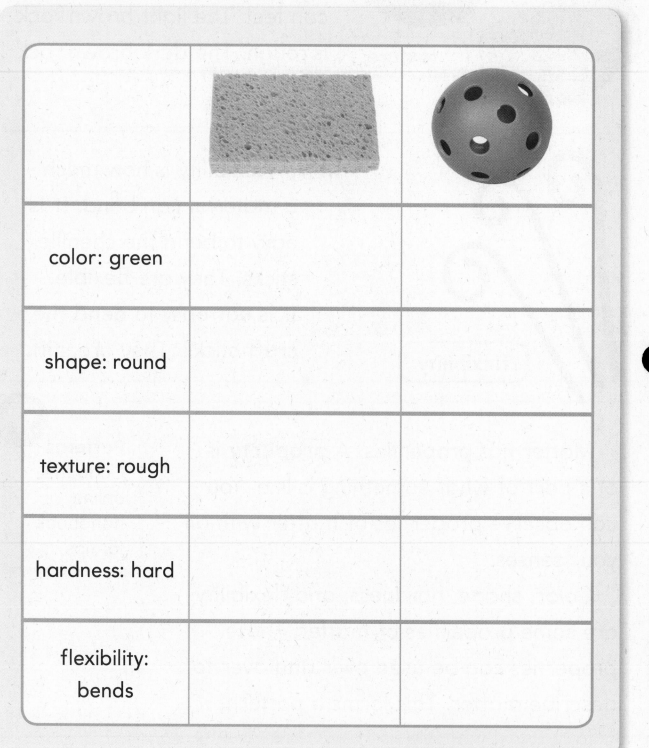

color: green		
shape: round		
texture: rough		
hardness: hard		
flexibility: bends		

Apply What You Know

Evidence Notebook • Can something have more than one property? Work with a partner to find out. Use all your **senses** to observe this box. Then, make a list to identify all properties of the box. Use evidence to support your answer. Record your answer in your Evidence Notebook.

States of Matter—Solids

Explore online. ▶

Look at the pictures to explore some solids.

A **solid** is a state of matter that keeps its shape. It will not change unless you do something to it, such as cut, bend, or break. A solid keeps its shape even when you move it. These properties can be used over and over to describe solids. This forms a pattern. Buildings, trucks, and chairs are all solids.

✏️▷ Draw a line under the words that tell what a solid is like.

🖐️ Apply What You Know

Evidence Notebook • Not all solids are hard. Solids can be soft like a cotton ball. What are some examples of soft solids? Discuss as a class. Use evidence to support your examples and record them in your Evidence Notebook.

States of Matter—Liquids

Explore online.

Look at the pictures to explore some liquids.

A **liquid** is a state of matter that does not have its own shape. It flows to take the shape of its container. The liquid in the tall glass has the same shape as the glass. If the liquid is poured into a wide bowl, the liquid takes the bowl's shape. These properties can be used over and over to describe liquids. This forms a pattern.

 Circle the words that tell what a liquid is like.

Apply What You Know

Work in a small group to investigate what happens when you shake a clear jar of water. Compare changes to the water and the jar. Identify patterns.

Planning and Carrying Out Investigations
Go to the online handbook for tips.

© Houghton Mifflin Harcourt

Which Materials Are Best?

A bike has parts made from rubber, metal, and foam. Why were these materials picked for the bike?

Cause and Effect
Go to the online handbook for tips.

Explore online.

foam seat
The seat is foam. Foam is soft, but firm enough to hold the weight of a rider. These properties of foam make the seat comfortable.

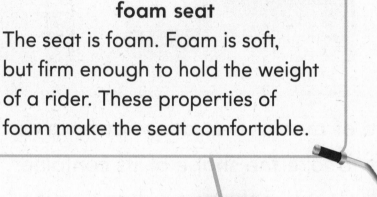

rubber tires
These tires are rubber. Rubber is strong and flexible. These properties of rubber give bike tires a smooth ride.

metal frame
The frame is metal. Metal is strong and hard. These properties of metal help the bike keep its shape.

Hands-On Activity

Engineer It • Explore Properties of Matter

Materials
_____

_____

Ask a Question

_____

Test and Record Data [Explore online. ▶]

Step 1

Observe the properties of each material. Compare the shape, texture, hardness, and flexibility of each one. Record your observations.

Material 1	Material 2	Material 3	Material 4

Step 2
Make a plan to test each material
to find out if it is a good pillow filler.

Step 3
Follow the steps of your plan to test each
one. Record and compare the results of each
material tested.

Data Recording Chart

Material 1	Material 2	Material 3	Material 4

Step 4
Analyze your results. Look for patterns.

Make a claim that answers your question.

_____

_____

What is your evidence?

_____

_____

Do the Math! • Which material made the better pillow filler? Make a bar graph to show the number of properties that each material had. Which one was liked best? Use the graph to answer the question.

Display Data
Go to the online handbook for tips.

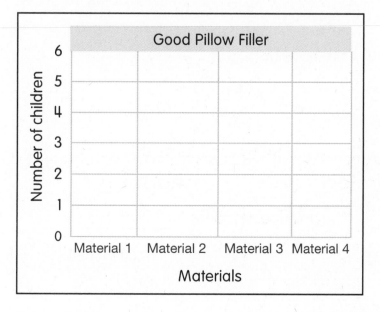

Which material did your class like best?
Use data from your bar graph as evidence.

_____

_____

Evidence Notebook • Think of other questions you have about the properties of materials. Record your work in your Evidence Notebook.

Apply What You Know

Read, Write, Share! • How can you describe an object's properties? Choose an object at home or in your classroom. Then write words to complete the riddle.

Recall Information
Go to the online handbook for tips.

This object is _____ and_____.
                  [color]   [shape]

It has a _____ surface that is _____.
              [texture]   [hardness]

It is also _____.
      [another property]

What is it? _____

Read your riddle to a partner. Can your partner answer the riddle?

Take It Further

Explore more online.

• Another Kind of Matter

People in Science & Engineering •
Dr. Eugene Tssui

Explore online. ▶

Meet Dr. Eugene Tssui. Dr. Tssui is an architect. An architect designs homes and other buildings.

When Dr. Tssui designs homes and buildings, he studies forms in nature, such as fish fins. He bases many designs on what he finds out. Look for the fish fin in the design of the house.

Dr. Eugene Tssui

This is the inside of the house.

What does the design of this house look like?

Dr. Tssui's Designs

Draw a line to match each building to the natural form on which it is based.

Patterns
Go to the online handbook for tips.

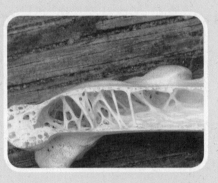

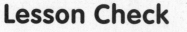

Can You Explain It?

 What is another use for rubber?

Be sure to

- Describe the properties of rubber.

- Name the object you would make using rubber.

- Explain why these properties make rubber good to use for your object.

_____

_____

_____

_____

Self Check

1. Which properties describe a cotton ball?
   Choose all correct answers.

   Ⓐ soft

   Ⓑ rough

   Ⓒ stiff

   Ⓓ round

2. Look at the pictures. What pattern
   do you see?

   Ⓐ A liquid keeps its shape.

   Ⓑ A liquid takes the shape of
   its container.

   Ⓒ A liquid spreads out to fill
   its container.

3. What are the properties of each vase? The vases
   may share some of the same properties.

	color	shape	texture	flexibility

4. Which pictures show a liquid? Circle each one.

....

5. What is a solid? What is a liquid? Write **solid** or **liquid** to make each sentence true.

Matter that keeps its shape is called a _____.
Matter that flows to take the shape of its container is called a _____.

....

6. Answer this riddle. This object is yellow and crescent-shaped. It has smooth skin that you can peel off. Its insides are soft and sweet to eat. What is it?

Ⓐ a lemon

Ⓑ the moon

Ⓒ a banana

Many objects are made up of smaller pieces.

By the End of This Lesson

I will be able to explain how an object made up of smaller pieces can be taken apart and put together to make a different object.

Taking Apart, Putting Together

What pieces do you see in the first object?
You can take this object apart. You can put the
same pieces together to make a different object.

Explore online.

Can You Explain It?

How did the first object become
a different one?

_____

_____

_____

_____

_____

Build It Up, Break It Down

Look at these materials.

Explore online. ▶

15 bricks

1 door

2 windows

You can make new objects from smaller pieces. Use the materials to make a house. Then compare your house to the houses your classmates made. How are your houses alike? How are they different?

✏️▷ Draw your house. Show the materials.

Which smaller pieces make up this chair? Choose all correct answers.

(A) legs

(B) seat

(C) arms

(D) back

(E) top

 Apply What You Know

Evidence Notebook • How can different objects be made from the same set of pieces? Work with a partner to discuss what makes up different objects, such as your homes. Use evidence to support your answer. Record your answer in your Evidence Notebook.

Constructing Explanations • Energy and Matter Go to the online handbook for tips.

What Is the Same?

Observe the two toy buildings.
How are they the same?
Choose the best answer.

(A) They are the same size.

(B) They are the same shape.

(C) They are made from the
same set of pieces.

Apply What You Know

**Read, Write, Share! • Evidence
Notebook** • Work with your class.
Discuss the smaller pieces that
make up a wooden bench. What
else could you build with the
same set of pieces? Use evidence
to support your discussion. Record
your answers in your Evidence
Notebook.

**Constructing
Explanations •
Energy and
Matter • Gather
Information** Go
to the online
handbook for tips.

Hands-On Activity
Build Objects from Smaller Pieces

Materials

_____

Ask a Question

_____

Test and Record Data Explore online. ▶

Step 1

Make a plan to find out how many objects you can build from the same set of smaller pieces.

_____

_____

_____

Step 2

Make observations as you follow your plan. Draw to record each object you build.

Step 3

Record the number of objects you build.

_____

_____

Step 4

Analyze your results.

Make a claim that answers your question.

_____

_____

_____

What is your evidence?

_____

_____

_____

_____

Take It Further
Careers in Science & Engineering •
Architect

Explore more online.

• What's Old Is New Again

Explore online. ▶

Architects plan and draw design ideas. They make models to show how their structures will look.

Architects work with others to improve their designs. They think of ways to make structures that are safe and strong.

Architects use sets of smaller pieces to build different models. They plan and design many types of structures, including houses, schools, and workplaces. Architects use art, math, and science in their work.

Design It!

Now it is your turn to be an architect.

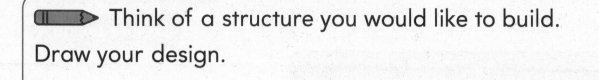 Think of a structure you would like to build. Draw your design.

Do the Math! • Kayla is building a model of her structure. Its base is a layer of square blocks that are all the same size. This drawing shows the red blocks Kayla is using. She wants to use blue blocks to fill the rest of the base.

How many blue blocks does Kayla need to finish the base?

Ⓐ 4

Ⓑ 12

Ⓒ 30

Partition Shapes
Go to the online handbook for tips.

Lesson Check

Name _____

Explore online. ▶

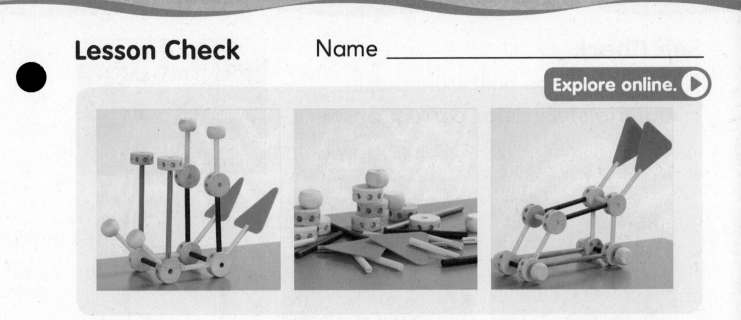

Can You Explain It?

✏️➤ How did the first object become a different one? Be sure to

- Explain how the first object is made up of a small set of pieces that can be taken apart.
- Explain how the same pieces can be put back together to make the new object.
- Use evidence to support your answer.

_____

_____

_____

_____

_____

Self Check

1. What could be built from these materials? Circle all correct answers.

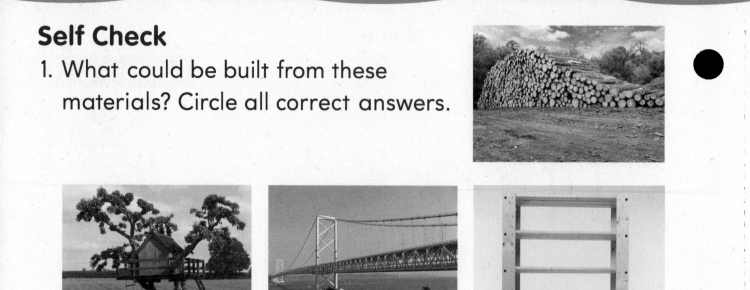

---

2. An object is made up of four legs and a flat top. What could it be? Choose all correct answers.

(A) rug

(A) desk

(C) lamp

(D) table

---

3. You built a house with blocks. Now you want to use the blocks to build something else. What is the first step you take?

(A) Take the house apart to get the blocks.

(B) Add blocks to your house.

(C) Put the blocks together in a new way.

4. How can you build this object? Number the pictures **1, 2,** and **3** to show the correct order.

_____   _____   _____

5. You take apart a bicycle. Which are part of the small set of pieces that make it up? Choose all correct answers.

Ⓐ seat

Ⓑ tires

Ⓒ engine

Ⓓ wipers

Ⓔ pedals

How Do Heating and Cooling Change Matter?

Matter can change in some interesting ways.

By the End of This Lesson

I will be able to tell how heating and cooling cause matter to change.

Matter Can Change

Look at the crayons. You use crayons to draw.
How are these crayons being used differently?

Explore online. ▶

Can You Explain It?

 What caused the crayons to change?

_____

_____

_____

Melt It

Explore online.

Investigate how adding heat by melting changes matter.

before   after

wax

butter

Heating can cause materials to change. Adding heat causes matter to melt, cook, and burn.

Adding heat to butter and wax will cause them to melt. When something **melts**, it changes from solid to liquid. Melting changes the state of matter. This is a pattern that happens when heat is added and something melts.

Think about the wax and butter.
What happened to the butter and
the wax when heat was added?

(A) They changed from solid to liquid.

(B) They changed from liquid to solid.

(C) They changed color.

Apply What You Know

Evidence Notebook • Work with
a partner to identify three examples
of changes to materials caused by
melting. How did adding heat
change the material? Use evidence
to tell how you know. Record your
answer in your Evidence Notebook.

**Engaging in
Argument from
Evidence**
Go to the online
handbook for tips.

Cook It

Explore online. ▶

Look at the pictures to see how adding heat by cooking changes matter.

before   after

pancake batter   pancake batter

chicken   chicken

Think about what happens to foods when they are cooked. Heat from the skillet was added to the pancake batter and the chicken. Both times, heat caused the foods to change in the same ways. This is a pattern that happens when heat is added and something cooks.

Which properties of the batter and the chicken changed when they were heated? Choose all correct answers.

(A) color

(B) flexibility

(C) texture

 Do you see any patterns in what happens when foods are cooked? If so, what are they? Record your answer.

_____

Apply What You Know

Evidence Notebook • Work with a partner to draw two examples of changes to materials by cooking. Be sure to show the material before and after heat was added. Do you see any patterns in how cooking changed the materials? Use evidence to support your answer. Record it in your Evidence Notebook.

Cause and Effect
Go to the online handbook for tips.

Burn It

Explore online.

Look at the pictures to see how adding heat by burning changes matter.

before   after

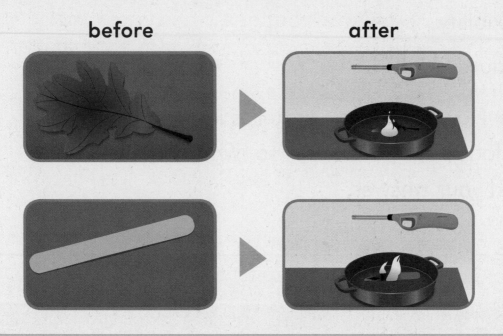

Heat from the flame is added to the wood and the leaf. This causes the materials to burn. Burning can also happen when you cook something too much. When something burns, heat changes its properties and makes it into another type of matter. This is a pattern that happens when heat is added and something burns.

What happened to the wood and the leaf when they were heated?

(A) They turned black and changed to ash.

(B) They changed from solids to liquids.

(C) They did not change.

Apply What You Know

Work with a small group to compare and contrast changes caused by melting, cooking, and burning in order to summarize what you know about how heat changes matter. Do you see any patterns in these changes?

✏️ Record your answer.

Cause and Effect • Patterns
Go to the online handbook for tips.

_____

_____

_____

_____

_____

Cool It Down

What happened to the water in this waterfall? Heat was taken away, and the water froze. When something **freezes**, it changes from a liquid to a solid.

Liquids such as milk, tea, and broth will freeze and change from a liquid to a solid. Freezing is a pattern that happens when enough heat is taken away.

Do the Math! • Compare the temperatures for Fairbanks, Alaska, and Miami, Florida. Write <, >, or = to compare the temperatures.
Fairbanks ___ Miami

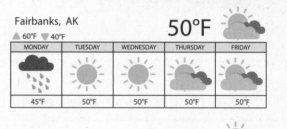

Fairbanks, AK   ▲60°F ▼40°F   50°F

MONDAY	TUESDAY	WEDNESDAY	THURSDAY	FRIDAY
45°F	50°F	50°F	50°F	50°F

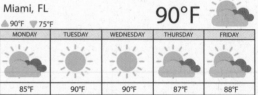

Miami, FL   ▲90°F ▼75°F   90°F

MONDAY	TUESDAY	WEDNESDAY	THURSDAY	FRIDAY
85°F	90°F	90°F	87°F	88°F

Apply What You Know

Evidence Notebook • Identify two materials to cool by freezing overnight. What patterns in how cooling changed these materials do you see? Use evidence to tell how you know, and record it in your Evidence Notebook.

Cause and Effect
Go to the online handbook for tips.

Hands-On Activity
Explore Cooling

Materials _____

_____

Ask a Question

_____

Test and Record Data   [Explore online. ▶]

Step **1**

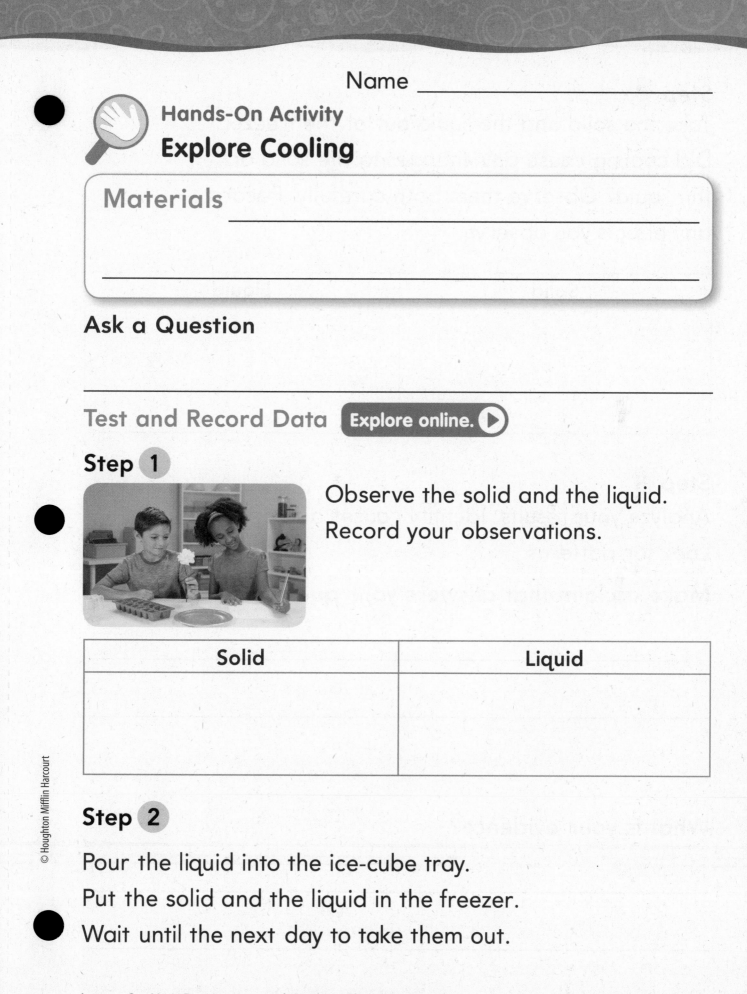

Observe the solid and the liquid.
Record your observations.

Solid	Liquid

Step **2**

Pour the liquid into the ice-cube tray.

Put the solid and the liquid in the freezer.

Wait until the next day to take them out.

Step 3

Take the solid and the liquid out of the freezer. Did cooling cause any changes to the solid or the liquid? Observe them both carefully. Record any effects you observe.

Solid	Liquid

Step 4

Analyze your results. Identify causes and effects. Look for patterns.

Make a claim that answers your question.

_____

_____

_____

What is your evidence?

_____

_____

Take It Further

Careers in Science & Engineering •
Chefs at Work

Explore more online.
- Changes All Around
- Find a Recipe

Chefs use math and science every day in their work. Chefs measure ingredients when they prepare food. When chefs cook, they have to know the right temperature to use for each food.

Explore online.

Chefs can add heat to change food. Adding heat can cause food to cook, to melt, or even to burn. The heat from the flame causes the sugar on top of the dessert to turn brown. It also causes the top to become hard.

Ask a Chef

Read, Write, Share!

What questions would you ask a chef about using heat?

Ask and Answer Questions
Go to the online handbook for tips.

> Draw or write to record your questions.

_____

_____

_____

_____

Get answers to your questions by asking a chef. Or, you can ask a cafeteria worker or an adult who likes to cook. Write about what you learn.

Lesson Check

Name _____

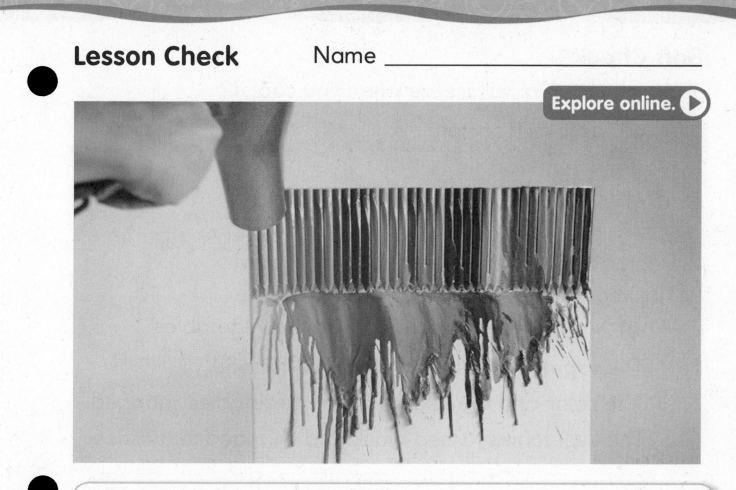

Can You Explain It?

 What caused the crayons to change?

Be sure to:

• Tell whether the crayons were heated or cooled.

• Describe how the crayons changed.

• Explain what caused the crayons to change.

_____

_____

_____

_____

Self Check

1. Which material will freeze when you cool it?

Ⓐ a plastic milk carton

Ⓑ a glass milk bottle

Ⓒ milk in a glass

2. Hector cooked some vegetables on a stove.
The vegetables became soft and brown.
What was the effect of cooking on the vegetables?

Ⓐ The vegetables turned from liquid to solid.

Ⓑ The color and the texture of the vegetables changed.

Ⓒ The vegetables turned black and changed into ashes.

3. Look at the snow and wax. What patterns do you see?

Ⓐ The materials changed from liquid to solid.

Ⓑ The materials changed from solid to liquid.

Ⓒ The materials turned black and changed into ashes.

4. Elizabeth places juice in a freezer. The next day she observes that the juice is frozen. What evidence does Elizabeth have to make the argument that the juice froze?

Ⓐ The juice changed from liquid to solid.

Ⓑ The juice changed from solid to liquid.

Ⓒ The juice changed in color only.

5. What happens when heat is added to wax? Choose all true statements.

Ⓐ It melts.

Ⓑ It changes from solid to liquid.

Ⓒ It changes to ashes.

6. What does burning cause wood to turn into?

Ⓐ black ashes

Ⓑ a liquid

Ⓒ ice

7. What would happen to a plastic bag if you put it into the freezer?

Ⓐ The bag would change to ashes.

Ⓑ The bag would change to a liquid.

Ⓒ The bag would stay solid.

Matter can change in ways that cannot be undone.

By the End of This Lesson

I will be able to explain that some changes to matter can be undone, but other changes cannot.

© Houghton Mifflin Harcourt

Fire It Up

Look at the pictures to explore what heat does to matter. What happens to wood when you burn it?

Explore online. ▶

before

during

after

Can You Explain It?

✏️ Can ashes be changed back into wood?

_____

_____

_____

_____

Reversible Changes

What happens to lemonade if you put it in the freezer overnight? How does it change? How does it stay the same? Let's find out.

Explore online. ▶

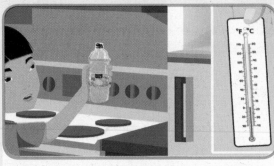

kitchen temperature 70°F

The boy has lemonade in a bottle. It is a liquid at room temperature. He puts the lemonade in the freezer overnight.

freezer temperature 1°F

The next morning the lemonade is a solid. The cold caused it to freeze. What will happen to the frozen lemonade if the boy leaves it out on the counter?

kitchen temperature 70°F

The next morning the change was undone. The lemonade had become liquid again. A change that can be undone, or reversed, is a **reversible** change. Freezing and melting can be reversible changes.

How does the lemonade change in each picture? Write to describe what happens.

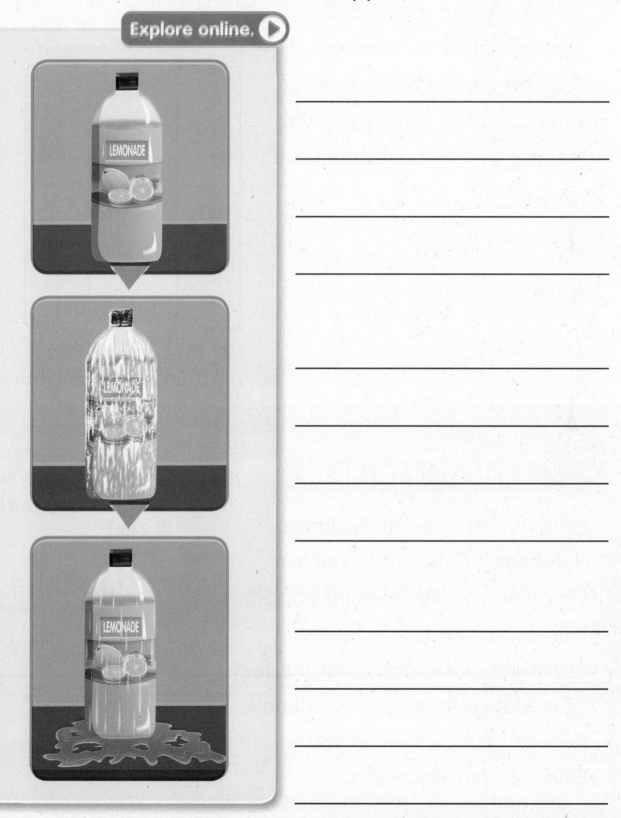

_____

_____

_____

_____

_____

_____

_____

_____

_____

_____

_____

Do the Math! • A thermometer measures temperature in units called degrees. How much warmer is the room temperature than the freezer temperature? Which number sentence could you use to answer the question?

Ⓐ 70 − 10 = ☐

Ⓑ 1 + 70 = ☐

Ⓒ 70 − 1 = ☐

Solve Word Problems
Go to the online handbook for tips.

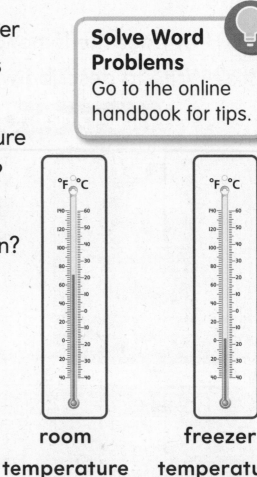

room temperature   freezer temperature

Apply What You Know

Read, Write, Share! • Evidence Notebook • Talk with a partner. What do you think would happen to milk if you put it in a freezer overnight? Use facts from the text as evidence to tell how you know. Record your answer in your Evidence Notebook.

Describe How Reasons Support a Text
Go to the online handbook for tips.

Irreversible Changes

Explore online.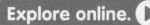

What happens to different materials when you cook, burn, or freeze them?

cooking

The raw vegetables are firm and dry. During cooking, they get softer, wet, and begin to turn brown. The cooked vegetables cannot change back into raw ones.

burning

The paper is white and in one piece. As the paper burns, it crumbles into powdery, gray ashes. The ashes cannot change back into a white piece of paper.

freezing

When the flower is frozen, its petals are cold and hard. Freezing the flower causes its shape to change. This change cannot be undone.

Some materials can be changed forever. A change that cannot be reversed, or undone, is an **irreversible** change.

Apply What You Know

Evidence Notebook • You have found out about irreversible changes to matter. Work with a small group to think about other materials you could change by cooking or burning. Describe the materials before they are cooked or burned. Then, describe them after being cooked or burned. Identify patterns in how cooking or burning changed all these materials. Use evidence to support your answer. Record your answer in your Evidence Notebook.

Cause and Effect • Patterns
Go to the online handbook for tips.

cook

burn

Name _____

Explore Changes to Matter

Materials

_____

_____

Ask a Question

_____

Test and Record Data Explore online. ▶

Step 1

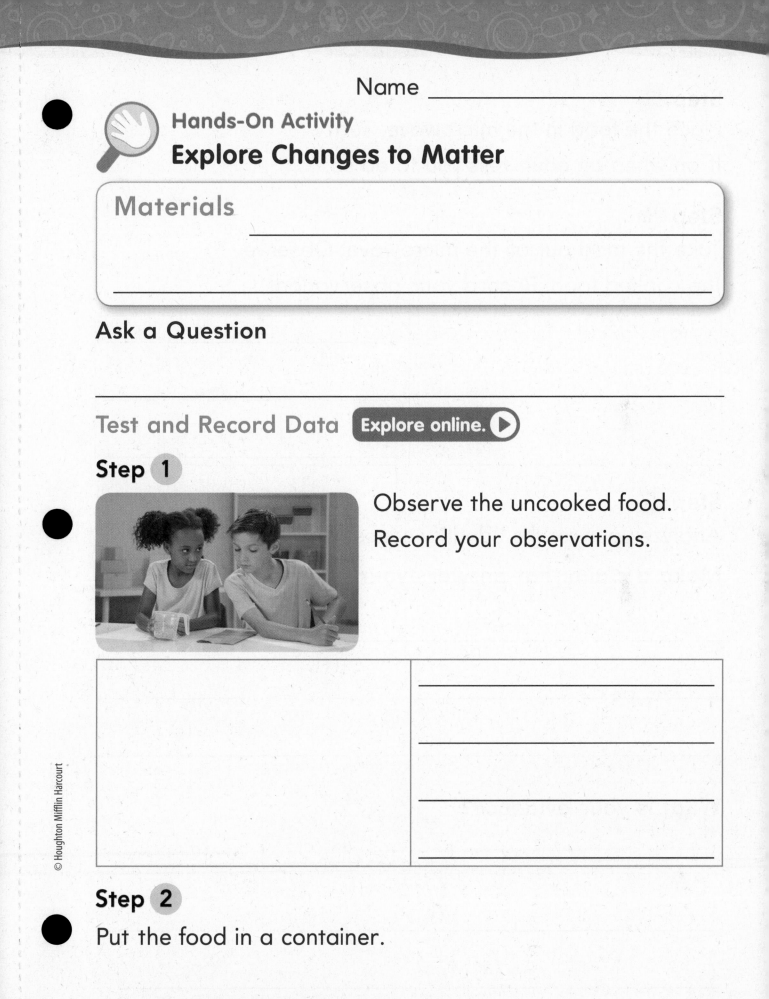

Observe the uncooked food.

Record your observations.

Step 2

Put the food in a container.

Step 3

Place the food in the microwave. Turn
it on when an adult tells you to do so.

Step 4

Take the food out of the microwave. Observe
the cooked food. Record your observations.

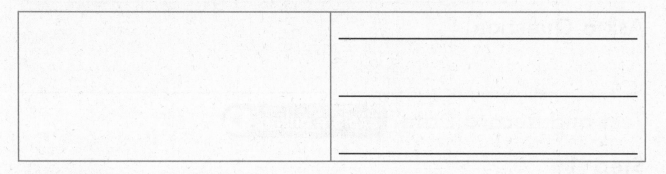

Step 5

Analyze your results. Identify causes and effects.

Make a claim that answers your question.

_____

_____

_____

What is your evidence?

_____

_____

_____

Take It Further
How Foods Change

Explore more online.

• Dissolve It

What changes happen to apples, avocados, and bananas after you cut them and leave them out on the counter?

Explore online. ▶

How Did the Foods Change?

How has the fruit changed? Is this change reversible? How do you know? Use evidence from the picture to support your answer.

Cause and Effect
Go to the online handbook for tips.

_____

_____

_____

_____

_____

Lesson Check

Name _____

before   during   after

Explore online. ▶

Can You Explain It?

 Can ashes be changed back into wood?

Be sure to:

• Describe how the wood changed.

• Tell what caused the wood to change.

• Explain whether this change is reversible or irreversible.

_____

_____

_____

_____

Self Check

1. What evidence do the pictures give to show that this change is reversible?

Ⓐ Freezing changes the juice pop into a different kind of material.

Ⓑ Adding heat to the juice pop makes it turn brown and melt.

Ⓒ The material in the juice pop stays the same even when its form changes.

2. What causes matter to change in each photo? Use a word from the box to identify each change.

cooking
burning
melting

burning   cooking   melting

3. Which are irreversible changes? Choose all that apply.

Ⓐ a fire burning in a fireplace

Ⓑ a melting ice-cream cone

Ⓒ muffins baking in the oven

Ⓓ a frozen lake in the winter

4. How do you know if a change is irreversible? Choose all that apply.

Ⓐ The material changes from a solid to a liquid.

Ⓑ The material becomes a different type of material.

Ⓒ The material can never go back to the way it was before the change.

Ⓓ The material stays the same type of material.

5. Read each cause and effect in the chart. Which changes are reversible? Which changes are irreversible? Write **reversible** or **irreversible** to identify each change.

Cause	Effect	Change
Fire burns wood.	Wood turns to ashes.	Irreversible
Freezer freezes lemonade.	Lemonade turns to solid.	reversible
Heat cooks vegetables.	Vegetables shrink, soften, and turn brown.	Irreversible
Heat cooks popcorn kernels.	Kernels turn white and fluffy.	irreversible

Unit 2 Performance Task
Engineer It • Build a Model Boat

Materials

_____

_____

STEPS

Step 1

Define a Problem You want to build a model boat that will float on water and will move by wind.

Step 2

Plan and Build You will need to think about materials, come up with ideas, and then build a boat.

Step 3

Test and Improve Test your design. Does your boat float and move? How can you improve your design?

Step 4

Redesign Make changes to the materials to make the boat better.

Step 5

Communicate Explain which materials make up your boat and why you chose them. Describe how putting the materials together made them do things that each one could not do by itself.

✔ Check

_____ I built a boat that floats and moves by wind.

_____ I tested my model boat design.

_____ I redesigned my model boat to make it work better.

_____ I shared my design with others.

Name _____

1. What happens to water when it freezes?
   Ⓐ It only changes color.
   Ⓑ It changes to a liquid.
   Ⓒ It changes to a solid.

2. How does matter change when it melts?
   Ⓐ It changes from a liquid to ashes.
   Ⓑ It changes from a solid to a liquid.
   Ⓒ It changes from a liquid to a solid.

3. Look at the wax and the muffin batter.
   Which statements are true? Choose all
   correct answers.

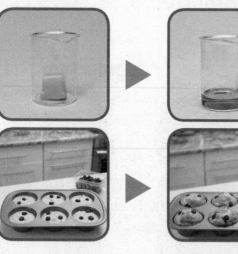

before   after

   Ⓐ Heat caused the wax to melt.
   Ⓑ Heat caused the muffin batter to cook.
   Ⓒ Heat caused the wax and muffin batter
      to burn and turn to ashes.

4. How will each container change when placed in a freezer? Choose all the containers that will not freeze.

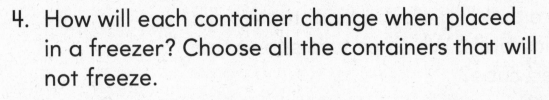

Ⓐ　　　　Ⓑ　　　　Ⓒ

5. Which objects are solids? Choose all correct answers.

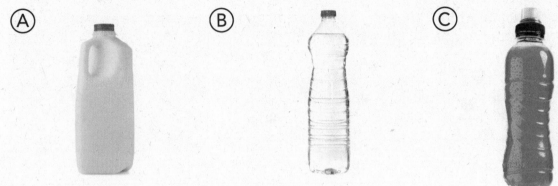

Ⓐ　　　　Ⓑ　　　　Ⓒ

6. Which are properties of the pencil? Choose all correct answers.
Ⓐ flexible
Ⓑ hard
Ⓒ yellow

7. Which change is irreversible?
Ⓐ candle burning
Ⓑ butter melting
Ⓒ water freezing

8. You are building a cube from toothpicks and clay balls. Which picture shows the finished cube?

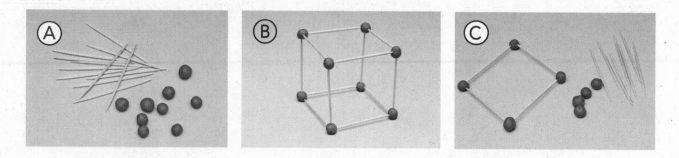

Ⓐ   Ⓑ   Ⓒ

9. What could be built from these materials? Choose all correct answers.

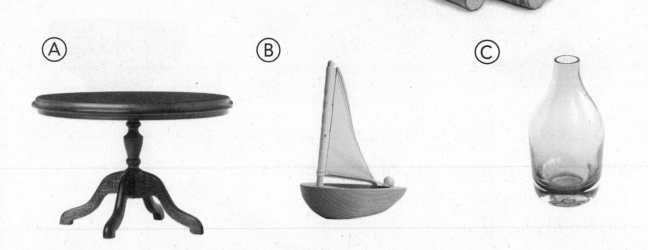

Ⓐ   Ⓑ   Ⓒ

10. Which are properties of the ball? Choose all correct answers.
    Ⓐ bends
    Ⓑ green
    Ⓒ round

Unit 3
Environments for Living Things

Unit Project • Explore Habitats

Why do plants and animals live where they do? Investigate to find out.

Unit 3 At a Glance

Unit Vocabulary

nutrient anything that living things, such as plants, need as food (p. 112)

pollen a sticky powder that flowers need to make seeds (p. 132)

habitat a place where living things get the food, water, air, and shelter needed to live (pp. 142, 158)

Vocabulary Game • Show the Word!

Materials
- 1 set of word cards
- paper
- pencils or other drawing tools

How to Play
1. Work with your partner to make word cards.
2. Place the cards face down on the table.
3. Pick a card, but do not show the word.
4. Draw or act out the word for your partner to guess.
5. When the word is guessed correctly, your partner picks a card to draw or act out.

Plants need certain things to live and grow.

By the End of This Lesson

I will be able to tell what a plant needs to grow and be healthy.

Plants Are Living Things

Explore online. ▶

Look at the pictures. What does a plant need?

Can You Explain It?

 What would happen if a plant does not get the things it needs?

_____

_____

_____

_____

_____

What Plants Need

Explore online. ▶

Look at the pictures to explore what plants need to live and grow.

water

air

nutrients

sunlight

space to grow

Plants need water, air, sunlight, nutrients, and space to grow. Plants get water from rain. People can also water plants. Plants use air, water, and sunlight to make their own food. Many plants also get nutrients from the soil. A **nutrient** is anything that living things, such as plants, need as food. Plants also need space so their roots and leaves have room to grow.

Which plant is getting everything it needs to live and grow? Circle Plant 1 or Plant 2.

Plant 1

Plant 2

Apply What You Know

Read, Write, Share! • **Evidence Notebook** • Look at the two pictures of the plants. Work in a small group to discuss what Plant 1 needs to look more like Plant 2. Identify patterns you observe. Use evidence to support your answer. Record it in your Evidence Notebook.

Cause and Effect • Gather Information Go to the online handbook for tips.

Taking It In

Explore online.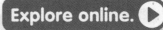

Look at the picture to explore the parts a plant has that help it get what it needs to live and grow.

Roots grow into the soil and hold a plant in place. The roots take in water and nutrients from the soil. Roots need space to grow.

A stem holds up a plant. A stem carries water and nutrients to other parts of a plant.

Leaves use sunlight, air, and water to make food for a plant. Leaves need space to grow so a plant can take in the air and sunlight it needs.

Complete the sentences to tell what parts of a plant do. Use the words from the word bank.

roots   leaves   stem

The _____ take in air and sunlight.

The _____ carries water and nutrients through the plant.

The _____ take in water and nutrients.

Do the Math! • Mr. Baker has 2 rows of plants in his garden. If he puts 5 plants in each row, how many plants will he have to water in all?

_____ plants

Use Equal Groups
Go to the online handbook for tips.

Apply What You Know

Evidence Notebook • A plant that gets enough water is healthy. A plant that does not get enough water is dry and wilted. What happens if a plant gets too much water? It may droop, and its leaves may turn yellow.

Observe these plants. Work with a partner. Use evidence to support your answer. Record your answers in your Evidence Notebook.

© Houghton Mifflin Harcourt

Name _____

Hands-On Activity
Explore What a Plant Needs

Materials

_____

Ask a Question

_____

Test and Record Data   Explore online.

Step 1

Pour water into each cup. Add red food coloring
to one of the cups and stir. Place one plant in each
cup. Leave the plants in the cups until the next day.

Step 2

Observe the plants.
Record your observations.

Step 3

Observe the plants in each cup.
Record any effects you observe.

Plant 1	Plant 2

Step 4

Analyze your results. Identify causes and effects.
Look for patterns.

Make a claim that answers your question.

_____

_____

_____

What is your evidence?

_____

_____

_____

Take It Further
Where Plants Grow

Explore more online.

• Growing Plants Without Soil

North America has many climates, or patterns of weather. Tundras, deserts, and wetlands all have different climates and plants.

Explore online. ▶

A tundra has short, cool summers and long, cold winters. Most plants grow close together and low to the ground to protect against the cold and the wind.

tundra

desert

Alaska (U.S.)

Canada

United States

Mexico

wetlands

A desert is dry. In some deserts, temperatures can go from hot to cold within one day. Many plants have thick stems or waxy leaves that store water for times when it is dry.

Wetlands are hot and humid with a lot of rain. Plants here grow well in very wet soil or water.

✏️ Where does each plant live? Label the pictures using the words in the box.

desert   tundra   wetlands

Name _____

Explore online. ▶

Can You Explain It?

✏️➤ What would happen if a plant does not get the things it needs?

Be sure to

• Describe how the plant might look.

• Explain what could happen if the plant continues to not get the things it needs.

_____

_____

_____

_____

Self Check

1. What do plants need to grow? Circle all correct answers.

2. Tyler and his family go away for two weeks. No one waters the plants while they are gone. What will the plants look like when they get home?

3. What do plants need to make food? Choose all correct answers.
   - (A) shelter
   - (B) sunlight
   - (C) air

4. What does each plant part do? Draw a line to match the picture of the plant part to the label that tells what it does.

| moves water through the plant | takes in sunlight and air to make food | takes in water and nutrients from the soil |

---

5. Why did the celery in the picture turn red?

Ⓐ The celery plant was kept in the dark.

Ⓑ The water moved up the stem into the leaves.

Ⓒ The celery plant did not get enough nutrients.

Engineer It • How Do Plants Depend on Animals?

Plants depend on animals in many ways.

By the End of This Lesson

I will be able to explain how plants depend on animals to help move seeds and pollen.

How Animals Help Plants

Look at the bee on the flower. The flower is providing the bee with nectar. How is the bee helping the plant?

Explore online. ▶

Can You Solve It?

 You want to add more flowers to your garden. How can bees help solve this problem?

_____

_____

_____

Animals Help Spread Seeds

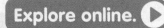 Explore online. ▶

Look at the pictures to explore how animals can help some plants spread their seeds.

Some plants have seeds covered in hooks and spines called burrs. These burrs hook onto an animal's fur. Over time, the burrs fall off. New plants may grow from the seeds.

Birds eat seeds and fruits that have seeds in them. They fly away with seeds in their beaks. Some seeds drop to the ground. New plants grow from the seeds.

Squirrels gather and hide acorns to eat later. Sometimes they do not come back for the acorns they have buried. Now trees can grow from these seeds.

Draw a line to match each animal with the way it can move seeds.

Structure and Function
Go to the online handbook for tips.

Seeds are buried in the ground.

Seeds fall from its fur.

Seeds drop from its mouth or beak.

Apply What You Know

Read, Write, Share! • Have you ever walked through the woods and found burrs stuck to your socks? If so, you have moved seeds. Think about a time you moved seeds or how you might move seeds. Use drawings or other pictures to support your ideas.

✏️ Draw or write about your ideas.

Use Visuals
Go to the online handbook for tips.

_____

_____

_____

_____

Hands-On Activity

Engineer It • Plan and Build a Model Tool

Materials

_____

Ask a Question

_____

Test and Record Data   Explore online. ▶

Step 1

Make a plan to build a tool that will pick up and move different seeds. Record your plan.

Step 2

Select your materials. Draw to design a model of your tool. Then build your model.

© Houghton Mifflin Harcourt

Step 3

Test your tool to find out which seeds it can move.
Record your data.

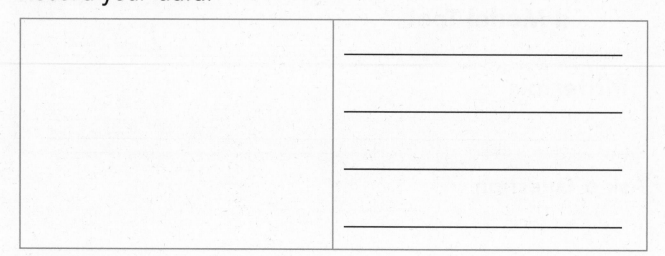

Step 4

Analyze your results. Identify how the shape
and structure of your tool affected how it worked.

Make a claim that answers your question.

_____

_____

_____

What is your evidence?

_____

_____

_____

Do the Math! • How many of each seed were you able to move with your tool? Graph your results.

Make a Bar Graph Go to the online handbook for tips.

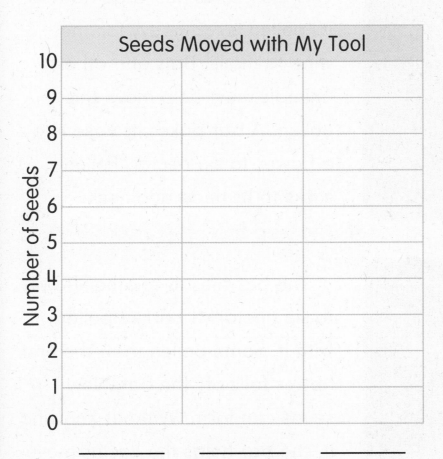

Look at your graph.

Which seeds were easy to move? _____

Which seeds were hard to move? _____

How Animals Spread Pollen

Explore online.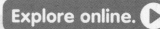

Look at the pictures to explore how animals, such as insects and bats, can help move pollen.

This tall cactus has large flowers. Its pollen is too heavy for the wind to move. Bats and other animals must help move this pollen. A bat pokes its nose into a flower to sip nectar. Pollen sticks to its head and neck.

The bat flies to another flower to sip nectar. It carries pollen with it. Some pollen from the first flower falls off the bat. New seeds can form. Without knowing it, the bat helps the cactus move pollen to make seeds.

Pollen is a sticky powder that flowers need to make seeds. Pollen must move from one flower to another for new seeds to form.

How does the bat help seeds form? Number each picture 1, 2, or 3 to show the correct order.

New flowers can grow.

_____

A bat gets pollen from the flower.

_____

The bat spreads pollen to other plants and new seeds form.

_____

Evidence Notebook • Work with a small group. Look at this sunflower. Tell how animals might help this flower. Give two examples as evidence to support your ideas. Record your answers in your Evidence Notebook. Share your group's ideas with your class.

Take It Further

Careers in Science & Engineering • Horticulturalist

Explore more online.

• Other Ways Seeds Travel

Explore online. ▶

Horticulturalists teach others how to care for plants. Some work with farmers. Others work at garden centers.

Horticulturalists are scientists who study plants and how they grow. These scientists find out what plants need to stay healthy. They study ways for plants to grow more fruit or vegetables. They help move pollen so plants can make seeds.

Horticulturalist

What Else Would You Like to Know?

Think of three questions you would like to ask a horticulturalist.

> ✏️ Draw or write to record your questions.

_____

_____

_____

Get answers to your questions by asking a horticulturalist. Or talk to someone who works at a garden center. Write about what you find out.

Explore online. ▶

Can You Solve It?

 You want to add more flowers to your garden. How can bees help solve this problem? Be sure to

- Tell what happens when a bee sips nectar.
- Describe what happens when the bee moves to a new flower.
- Explain how moving pollen helps plants.

_____

_____

_____

© Houghton Mifflin Harcourt • Image Credits: ©Semjonow Juri/Shutterstock

Self Check

1. What is the most likely way this seed is moved?

   Ⓐ A bird carries it in its mouth.

   Ⓑ It sticks to an animal's fur.

   Ⓒ A chipmunk buries it.

2. What can you find out from a model of a seed? Choose all correct answers.

   Ⓐ the size of the seed

   Ⓑ the shape of the seed

   Ⓒ the structure of the seed

3. Which type of seed does each animal move? Draw a line to match each animal with the type of seed it moves.

© Houghton Mifflin Harcourt • Image Credits: (tr) ©shantyboys/iStock/Getty Images Plus/Getty Images; (cl) ©Geoff du Feu/Alamy; (c) ©Eduardo Mariano Rivero/iStock; (cr) ©Vera Zinkova/Shutterstock; (bl) ©ideeone/iStockPhoto.com; (bc) ©Martin Novak/Shutterstock; (br) ©Holger Leue/Lonely Planet Images/Getty Images

4. What causes a bee to move pollen?
Choose the **best** answer.

Ⓐ The pollen is light and sticky.

Ⓑ The pollen has structures like wings.

Ⓒ The pollen has hooks that catch onto the bee.

5. A farmer sees that his strawberry crop is not as large as it was last year. He reads in the newspaper that there are fewer bees in the area. What conclusion can you draw about why his crop is smaller?

Ⓐ The crop grows better if bees do not move pollen.

Ⓑ The crop grows better if many bees move pollen.

Ⓒ The number of bees does not affect the crop.

What Plants and Animals Live in Water Habitats?

Many plants and animals live in a pond.

By the End of This Lesson

I will be able to compare plants and animals in different water habitats.

Water Habitats

Look at the pictures to explore some water habitats that plants and animals live in. How are they alike? How are they different?

pond

river delta

Explore online. ▶

tide pool

Can You Explain It?

✏️ Why do some plants and animals only live in ponds, in river deltas, or in tide pools?

_____

_____

_____

Ponds

Explore online.

● Most duckweed plants have no roots. They float on the water to get the sunlight they need.

● An iris's roots dig into the pond's bottom. Its leaves are above water to get sunlight.

● A dragonfly starts its life in the water, but lives on land as an adult. It eats flying insects.

● A crayfish uses gills to take in oxygen. It eats plants and animals.

● A sunfish lives in shallow water. It has gills and eats small animals.

● A tadpole is one stage in a frog's life. It has gills and eats plants and insects.

Most ponds are not very deep. They have fresh water, which is not salty. These are patterns. A pond can have many habitats. A **habitat** is a place where living things get the food, water, air, and shelter they need to live. Above water and below water are two kinds of habitats in a pond.

✏️ Circle the animals that live above the water. Put an X on the animals that live under the water.

✋ **Apply What You Know**

Evidence Notebook • With a partner, discuss what makes a pond a good place to live. Identify patterns. Use evidence to support your ideas. Record your answers in your Evidence Notebook.

💡 **Patterns** Go to the online handbook for tips.

© Houghton Mifflin Harcourt

River Deltas

Explore online. ▶

● A cypress tree's roots grow under and above the water. Water helps spread its seeds.

● A thalia's stems and leaves float on the water. Its roots dig into the river bottom to hold it in place.

● An alligator lives mostly in fresh water. Its lungs take in air. It hunts other animals.

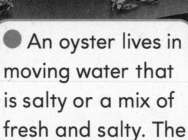

● A catfish lives in fresh water. It feeds mostly at night and uses its whiskers to find food on the river bottom.

● An oyster lives in moving water that is salty or a mix of fresh and salty. The moving water helps bring it food.

● This crab lives in a mix of fresh and salty water. It uses its gills to take in oxygen from the water.

A river delta forms when a river meets another body of water. In a river delta, there may be fresh water or a mix of fresh water and salty water. These are patterns. One type of habitat found in a river delta is above the water and the land around it. Another type is below the water.

Think about the type of water each animal needs in its habitat. Circle all animals that can live in water that is salty.

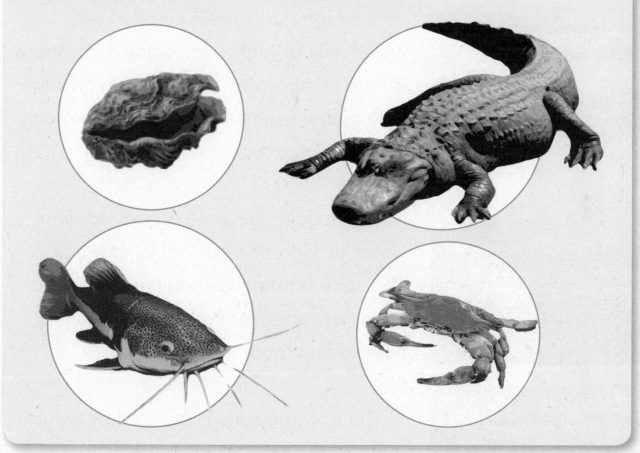

Apply What You Know

Evidence Notebook • With a partner, discuss why a river delta is a good place for some plants and animals to live. Record your answer in your Evidence Notebook.

Patterns
Go to the online handbook for tips.

Tide Pools

Tide pools have three parts called zones. Each zone is a habitat.

Explore online. ▶

The high tide zone is covered with water only at high tide. At low tide, there is little or no water. The animals that live in this zone usually have hard bodies or can hold onto rocks.

The middle tide zone is covered with water at high tide but not at low tide. This zone is home to many animals. That is why animals from other zones come here to find food.

The low tide zone is covered by water most of the time. Many animals that live in this zone use gills to take in oxygen from the water.

Twice a day, every day, the salty water at the ocean's shore rises and falls. At high tide, the water rises and covers the shore. At low tide, it falls back. It leaves pools of water between the rocks that are called tide pools. This is a pattern.

Very few plants live in the salty waters of a tide pool. Look at the picture to explore the many animals in the different tide zones.

Explore online. ▶

As this crab moves, the anemone on its shell finds food and uses its stingers to protect the crab.

Coral often grow in groups and stay in one place. They collect food as it floats by.

A sea urchin has sharp spines to protect it. It uses its spines to move and to catch food.

A zebra blenny can jump from pool to pool to escape danger. It eats plant-like algae.

This shrimp eats tiny living things that grow on fish. When it is hungry, it dances to let the passing fish know.

This worm has gills that look like feathers. It uses its gills to take in oxygen from the water and trap food.

✏️ Think about where each animal lives in a tide pool. Match each animal with its correct location.

middle tide zone

high tide zone

low tide zone

🖐 **Apply What You Know**

Read, Write, Share! • Research the plants and animals that live in a water habitat close to you. Identify patterns. Make a poster of these plants and animals.

💡 **Participate in a Research Project • Patterns** Go to the online handbook for tips.

Name _____

Make Model Habitats

Materials

_____

Ask a Question

_____

Test and Record Data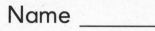

Step 1

Make a plan to build your model habitats. Identify plants and animals that live in the habitat. Record your plan.

_____

_____

Step 2

Set up your habitats by filling your container with rocks, plants, and animals.

Step 3

Add water to your model. Observe your tide pool. Record your observations.

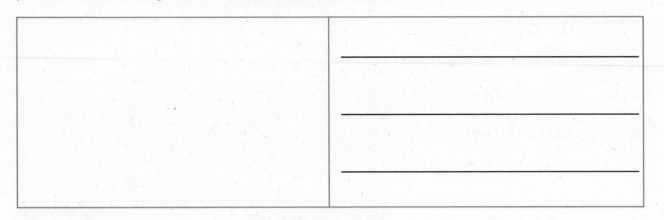

Step 4

Analyze your results. Make comparisons.
Identify patterns.

Make a claim that answers your question.

_____

_____

_____

What is your evidence?

_____

_____

_____

Take It Further

Careers in Science & Engineering •
Marine Biologist

Explore more online.
• Coral Reefs

Marine biologists are scientists. They study living things in oceans and other bodies of salt water.

Explore online. ▶

These marine biologists study animals in a tide pool. They keep track of the animals they see. They look for reasons that the numbers of some animals are low.

Marine biologists care about the environment. They want people to care, too. They teach people about plants and animals that live in different marine habitats.

✏️ Draw a line under the sentences that tell what a marine biologist does.

© Houghton Mifflin Harcourt • Image Credits: (cl) ©Jonathan Blair/Corbis Documentary/Getty Images; (br) ©Kip Evans/Design Pics/Perspectives/Getty Images; (tr) ©Moment Video RF/Getty Images

Do the Math! • A marine biologist counted the number of animals in a tide pool. Use the data in the tally chart to complete the picture graph.

Make a Picture Graph Go to the online handbook for tips.

Tide Pool Animals	
Animal	Tally
clam	卌 I
coral	卌
crab	IIII
sea star	III

Tide Pool Animals								
clam								
coral								
crab								
sea star								

Key: Each ⬭ stands for 1 animal.

How many animals did the marine biologist count in all? _____ animals

Lesson Check

Name _____

Explore online.

pond | river delta | tide pool

Can You Explain It?

Why do some plants and animals only live in ponds, in river deltas, or in tide pools?

Be sure to

• Describe where plants and animals live.

• Describe how they get what they need.

• Compare one plant or one animal from habitats found in ponds, river deltas, and tide pools.

_____

_____

_____

_____

Self Check

1. Where does each plant or animal live?
   Write the correct name for each place.

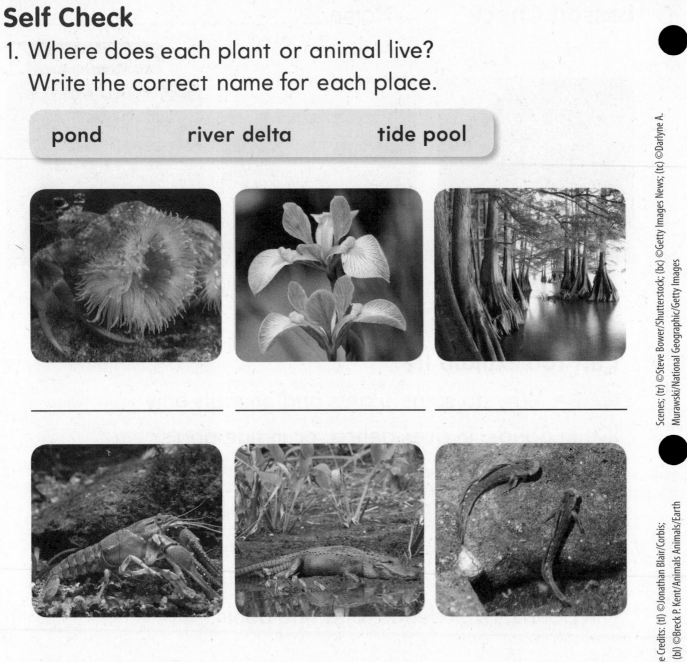

pond   river delta   tide pool

_____   _____   _____

_____   _____   _____

2. Which are **true** about tide pools? Choose all
   correct answers.

   Ⓐ A tide pool has many plants.

   Ⓑ Many freshwater animals live in a tide pool.

   Ⓒ Some tide pool animals move to different zones.

   Ⓓ The amount of water in a tide pool can change.

154

3. How are a cypress tree and duckweed alike and different? Choose all correct answers.

Ⓐ Both plants have large roots.

Ⓑ Only one of these plants floats on the water's surface.

Ⓒ Both plants live in habitats that provide everything they need to live.

Ⓓ Only one of these plants digs its roots into the muddy bottom of its habitat.

4. What makes a river delta a good place for an oyster to live? Choose all correct answers.

Ⓐ It can only survive deep underwater.

Ⓑ It needs moving water to bring food to it.

Ⓒ It can live in salty water or a mix of fresh and salty water.

5. Which are true about plants and animals that live in a pond?

Ⓐ The animals living in water have gills.

Ⓑ The plants and animals can live in fresh water.

Ⓒ The plants and animals get what they need to live and grow.

What Plants and Animals Live in Land Habitats?

Different kinds of plants and animals live in a rain forest.

By the End of This Lesson

I will be able to compare plants and animals in different land habitats.

Land Habitats

How are these places alike and how are they different?

rain forest

forest

savanna

Explore online. ▶

Can You Explain It?

Why do certain plants and animals only live in certain land habitats?

_____

_____

_____

_____

© Houghton Mifflin Harcourt • Image Credits: (l) ©Morley Read/age fotostock; c ©Artbeats/Corbis

Rain Forest Habitats

It is warm and wet all year long in a rain forest. Plants grow quickly. These are patterns. Look at the pictures to explore some habitats in a rain forest.

Explore online.

The canopy gets a lot of sunlight. Flowers and fruits fill the trees. Many animals that live here never leave the top of the trees.

The understory is shady. Plants that need little sun do well here. So do birds, small animals, and reptiles such as lizards and snakes.

The floor is dark and damp. There are many leaves, fallen fruits, and tree roots. Animals that eat insects live here.

A **habitat** is a place where a living thing gets the food, water, and shelter it needs.

How are these rain forest habitats alike?

Look at the picture to explore plants and animals that live in the rain forest canopy.

Explore online. ▶

● The tamarin uses its legs and claws to climb and jump. It eats fruit, small birds, and insects.

● A liana vine grows up a tree to reach sunlight. It has large leaves to take in sunlight.

● The sloth gets water from leaves and fruits it eats. Its sharp claws let it climb and hang upside-down.

● This tree frog has feet that can cling to leaves. Its sticky tongue catches insects.

● This orchid does not grow in soil. It grows on a tree to be close to the sunlight it needs.

● A harpy eagle has wings that are wide. It swoops down to grab animals with its sharp claws.

© Houghton Mifflin Harcourt

Look at the picture to explore plants and animals that live in the rain forest understory.

This butterfly's bad taste keeps birds away. The bad taste is from the leaves it ate as a caterpillar.

This plant can start life in a tree. Its roots grow down for support. Its vines grow up to take in sunlight.

Explore online. ▶

The boa blends in with the leaves. It lays on a branch and waits for a bird or lizard to pass by.

These ants have sharp jaws to cut leaves. They use the leaves to make food in their nests.

A bromeliad grows on other plants. Its leaves collect rain. Insects, snails, and tiny frogs live in the bromeliad.

The zebra plant can grow in soil or on a tree. It takes in nutrients and moisture through its leaves.

These animals live on the rain forest floor. Identify which patterns explain why they live there. Choose all correct answers.

Ⓐ They blend in well with this habitat.

Ⓑ They have claws for climbing trees.

Ⓒ They do well in a warm, wet habitat.

Ⓓ They find the food they need in this habitat.

✋ **Apply What You Know**

Evidence Notebook • Work with a partner. Explain why a rain forest is a good place for this iguana. Use evidence to support your ideas. Identify patterns. Record your answer in your Evidence Notebook.

💡 **Patterns** Go to the online handbook for tips.

Forest Habitats

In this forest, trees lose their leaves in the fall. They grow new ones in the spring. Many animals also change with the seasons. These are patterns. Look at the pictures to explore some habitats in a forest.

Explore online.

Sunlight comes through the trees to the forest floor. Bushes, wildflowers, and other plants can grow. Animals have food to eat and many places to take shelter.

The tree branches have many leaves, seeds, and nuts for animals to eat. In winter, the leaves fall. Animals may leave for warmer places. They may sleep for the winter or grow thick fur to stay warm.

How are these forest habitats alike?

© Houghton Mifflin Harcourt • Image Credits: (t) ©Artbeats/Corbis; (c) ©Artbeats/Corbis; (b) ©Radius Images/Alamy; (c) ©Gabby Salazar/National Geographic/Getty Images

Look at the picture to explore plants and animals that live on the forest floor.

Explore online. ▶

● A deer's brown fur can change to gray. This helps it blend in with the changing forest. It eats plants.

● This fox eats fallen fruit and hunts animals. It can even find animals under the snow.

● A skunk hunts at night. It eats insects and small animals. In winter, it stays in an underground den.

● Ferns grow in moist, shady places. They have long leaves. Ferns lose their leaves in fall.

● Moss can grow on tree trunks and rocks. It takes in water from its stem and leaves.

● An aster can grow in the shade. Its flowers bloom in the fall and may attract butterflies.

© Houghton Mifflin Harcourt

Look at the picture to explore plants and animals that live in the branches of trees.

● An opossum's diet changes with the seasons. It nests in tree holes but sleeps underground in winter.

● A hawk blends in with the trees. It builds a nest and stays in the forest all year. It hunts small animals.

Explore online. ▷

● A hickory tree has bark that makes a good home for some animals. It has nuts with hard shells that split open.

● A birch tree has smooth seeds that change from green to brown. The wind spins the seeds in the air.

● A beech tree has leaves that make good hiding places for small animals. Its fruits split open with beechnuts.

● Bald eagles hunt fish and small animals. They build nests near water. Eagles fly to warmer areas for the winter.

✏️ **What are three patterns you observed in the forest?**

_____

_____

_____

_____

_____

Apply What You Know

Evidence Notebook • Choose all animals that might live in a forest. Use evidence to support your answer. Record it in your Evidence Notebook.

arctic fox

toucan

black bear

chipmunk

monkey

cardinal

Savanna Habitats

A savanna has tall grasses with a few shrubs and trees. It has a rainy season and a dry season. It is warm all year. These are patterns. Look at the pictures to explore some habitats in a savanna.

Explore online. ▶

One savanna habitat is within the grasses. This is where small animals make their homes. These animals eat plants, insects, and seeds.

Each tree in the savanna is its own habitat. The trees have flowers and fruit. Some are a source of water for animals during the dry season.

 How are the savanna habitats alike?

Look at the picture to see plants and animals that live in the grasses of the savanna.

Explore online. ▶

● Buffalo grass can grow to 3 feet. It grows well in the dry season. Its seeds grow at the top of the plant.

● A springhare lives in a burrow. It eats roots, grasses, stems, seeds, and leaves.

● A pangolin has scales to keep it safe. It hunts ants and termites. It gathers them with its sticky tongue.

● Stinking grass has a bad smell and grows in clumps. Animals like the taste of its new leaves.

● A mongoose eats ants and termites in the dry season. It eats beetles and grasshoppers in the rainy season.

● Guinea grass has stems that grow to 6 feet. When the stems bend and touch the ground, roots and new plants grow.

Look at the picture to explore plants and animals that live in a baobab tree.

Explore online. ▶

● A bush baby makes its nest in the tree. It eats insects, fruit, and nectar. It licks water from the tree cracks.

● Bats visit the baobab tree at night. They sip nectar from the flowers and juice from the fruits.

● This parrot eats seeds, nuts, berries, fruit, and nectar. It eats seeds from the grasses during the dry season.

● A baobab tree loses its leaves in the dry season. It is full of leaves, flowers, and fruits in the rainy season. It stores water in its trunk.

● An elephant eats grasses, leaves, fruits, twigs, and bark. Its long trunk can pick a flower or rip a branch off a tree.

What things does the baobab tree provide for the animals? Choose all correct answers.

Ⓐ It provides food.

Ⓑ It provides shelter.

Ⓒ It provides water.

Apply What You Know

Evidence Notebook • Elephants live in the savanna. Explain why the savanna is a good place for an elephant to live. Identify patterns and use evidence in your answer. Record it in your Evidence Notebook.

Do the Math! • Draw bars in the graph to show how many animals you see in the savanna.

Display Data
Go to the online handbook for tips.

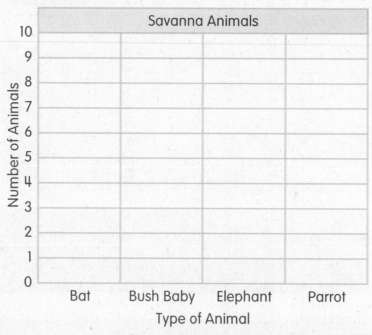

Savanna Animals

Number of Animals

10
9
8
7
6
5
4
3
2
1
0

Bat   Bush Baby   Elephant   Parrot

Type of Animal

Name _____

Hands-On Activity
Make a Habitat Exhibit

Materials
_____

Ask a Question

_____

Test and Record Data Explore online. ▶

Step 1

Make a plan to research and compare plants and animals that live in a habitat found in the savanna. Identify the habitat and record your plan.

_____

_____

Step 2

Research your plants and animals.
Record your observations. Make a poster.

_____

_____

Step 3

Set up your class exhibit. Compare the plants and animals in each habitat. Identify how they are alike and how they are different.

_____	Both	_____

Step 4

Analyze your results. Identify patterns.

_____

_____

Make a claim that answers your question.

_____

_____

What is your evidence?

_____

_____

Take It Further
People in Science & Engineering •
Dr. Emilio Bruna

Explore more online.
- Stepping on Habitats

Dr. Emilio Bruna is an ecologist. He studies how plants, animals, and people interact in an environment.

Explore online. ▶

Dr. Bruna travels to Brazil to study the Amazon rain forest. He makes observations of how people cause changes to the rain forest. He wants to find out how these changes affect the plants and animals that live there.

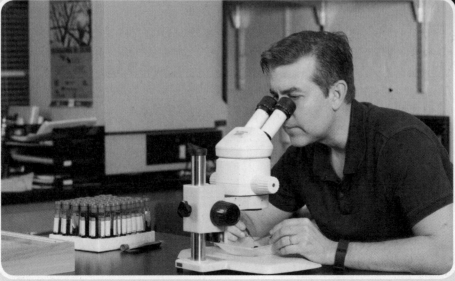

© Houghton Mifflin Harcourt

Read, Write, Share! • What questions do you have about Dr. Bruna's work? Record your questions. Gather information from different sources to answer your questions. Record your answers.

Participate in a Research and Writing Project Go to the online handbook for tips.

Write or draw to describe Dr. Bruna's studies.

Lesson Check

Name _____

Explore online. ▶

| rain forest | forest | savanna |

Can You Explain It?

✏️ Why do certain plants and animals only live in certain land habitats?

Be sure to

• Compare two plants or animals from a habitat.

• Describe how each plant or animal gets the things it needs.

• Explain why the plants or animals only live in that habitat.

_____

_____

_____

_____

_____

Self Check

1. Answer this riddle. I am a colorful bird. My big beak helps me crack open nuts that grow in the canopy of tall trees. Where do I live?

   Ⓐ in a forest

   Ⓑ in a rain forest

   Ⓒ in a savanna

2. Answer this riddle. My fur is thick and black. It keeps me warm in the cold winter. Where do I live?

   Ⓐ in a forest

   Ⓑ in a rain forest

   Ⓒ in a savanna

3. What are features of rain forests and forests? Use the words **rain forest** and **forest** to complete the sentences below.

   Habitats in a rain forest and in a forest both have trees. Because it is warm and wet all year, these plants grow thicker and taller in a

   _____.

   During the fall, the leaves fall off the trees in a

   _____.

4. Where does each plant or animal live?
Write the correct name for each place.

rain forest   forest   savanna

5. The zebra lives in the savanna. How does it get what it needs there?

Ⓐ It can get water from the plants it eats.

Ⓑ It can find the food it needs.

Ⓒ It can take shelter in an underground burrow.

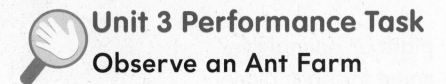
Materials

_____

_____

STEPS

Step 1

Use the tool to begin making a few tunnels in the ant farm. Then place the ants inside.

Step 2

Feed the ants a couple of food crumbs twice a week. Use a dropper to place a few drops of water every other day.

Step 3

Use a hand lens to observe the ants three times a week for two weeks.

Step 4

What did the ants do with the food you left? How do they build tunnels? What do ants do when they meet each other in the tunnels? Draw and write to record your observations.

Step 5

Compare your ant farm with the ant farms of your classmates. What patterns do you see?

 **Check**

_____ I observed my ants to see how they make tunnels and find food.

_____ I recorded my observations.

_____ I compared my ant farm with others to look for patterns.

1. What do plants need to live and grow?
    Choose all correct answers.

    Ⓐ air

    Ⓑ sunlight

    Ⓒ water

2. Which plant part takes in sunlight to make
    food?

    Ⓐ leaves

    Ⓑ roots

    Ⓒ stem

3. Sadie's plant does not look well.
    What does it need?

    Ⓐ soil

    Ⓑ shelter

    Ⓒ water

4. How do plants depend on animals? Choose all
    correct answers.

    Ⓐ They move plants from place to place.

    Ⓑ They move seeds so new plants can grow.

    Ⓒ They move pollen so plants can make seeds.

5. What can an animal find in its habitat? Choose all correct answers.
   Ⓐ food
   Ⓑ shelter
   Ⓒ water

6. What is **true** about a tide pool? Choose all correct answers.
   Ⓐ It has water that is salty.
   Ⓑ It has water that is fresh.
   Ⓒ It has water that rises and falls back.

7. Look at these pond plants. What patterns do you see?

   Ⓐ They both live underwater.
   Ⓑ The leaves of both plants are above the water.
   Ⓒ They both do not need sunlight.

8. Max reads about a plant that grows in a place that is warm and wet all year. Where does this plant most likely live?

Ⓐ forest

Ⓑ rain forest

Ⓒ savanna

9. Which is true about **both** a forest and a savanna?

Ⓐ They both have many trees.

Ⓑ They are both homes for elephants.

Ⓒ They both have different seasons.

10. Where does each animal live? Match each animal to where it lives.

Unit 4
Earth's Surface

Unit Project • Explore Ocean Water

Why does an ocean not freeze completely? Investigate to find out.

Unit 4 At a Glance

Unit Vocabulary

map a drawing or model of a place (p. 204)

map title part of a map that tells what the map shows (p. 205)

map key part of a map that shows what the map colors and symbols mean (p. 205)

compass rose part of a map that shows the directions north, south, east, and west (p. 205)

Vocabulary Game • Guess the Word

Materials
- 1 set of word cards

How to Play

1. Work with a partner to make word cards.
2. Place the cards face down in a pile.
3. One player picks the top card, but does not show it.
4. The second player asks questions to guess the word.
5. When the word is guessed correctly, the second player takes a card. Then, the first player asks questions to guess the word.

Water is found in many places on Earth.

By the End of This Lesson

I will be able to identify where water is found on Earth. I will be able to describe characteristics of bodies of water.

186

Bodies of Water

Water can be found in many places on Earth. Look at the pictures to explore some bodies of water.

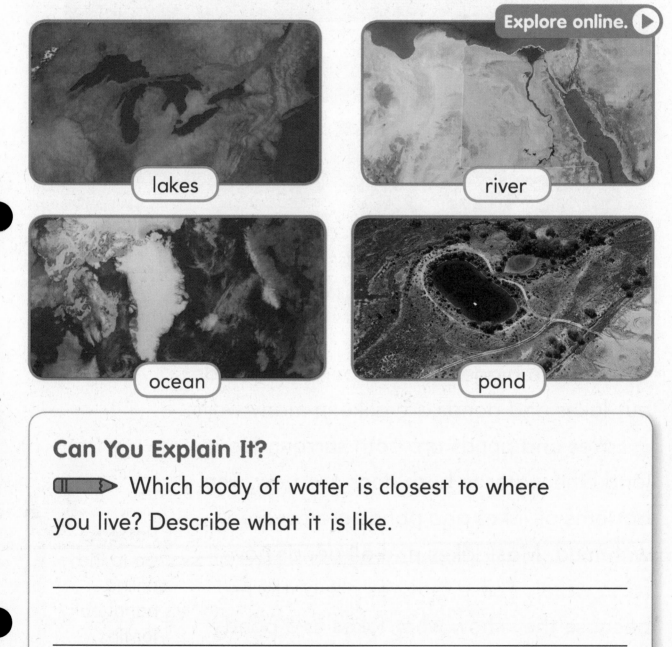

lakes

Explore online. ▶

river

ocean

pond

Can You Explain It?

✏️ Which body of water is closest to where you live? Describe what it is like.

_____

_____

© Houghton Mifflin Harcourt • Image Credits: (tl) ©JJMedia/Shutterstock; (tr) ©Yarr65/Shutterstock; (bl) ©OrlowskiDesigns/Shutterstock; (br) ©De Agostini Picture Library/Getty Images

Lakes and Ponds

Explore online. ▶

Look at the pictures to explore lakes and ponds.

lake

pond

Lakes are bigger and deeper than ponds, but lakes and ponds are alike in many ways.

Lakes and ponds are both surrounded by land. The water in both does not flow. The bottoms of lakes and ponds are covered with mud. Most lakes and all ponds have fresh water. These features are patterns because they show what lakes and ponds have in common.

Patterns
Go to the online handbook for tips.

● How are lakes and ponds alike?

Ⓐ They are both very deep.

Ⓑ They are both surrounded by land.

Ⓒ They are both made up of salt water.

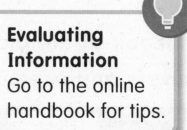

Evaluating Information
Go to the online handbook for tips.

 Apply What You Know

Measure 1 gallon of water and 1 tablespoon of water. The gallon stands for all water on Earth. The tablespoon stands for all fresh water that people can drink. How does the total amount of water on Earth compare to the amount of water that people can drink?

_____

_____

_____

© Houghton Mifflin Harcourt

Rivers and Oceans

Look at the pictures to explore rivers and oceans.

Explore online. ▶

river

ocean

Most rivers contain fresh water. Rivers may be wide or narrow. They all have land on two sides. Rivers begin on high ground. They flow downward into other rivers, lakes, and oceans. These features are patterns because they show what rivers have in common.

Oceans are the largest bodies of water on Earth. Ocean water is salty. Oceans cover most of Earth's surface and hold almost all its water. These features are patterns because they show what oceans have in common.

✏️ Write **oceans** or **rivers** to complete the following sentence:

There are different bodies of water.

_____ flow into _____ .

Label each picture using the terms in the box.

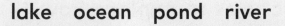
lake   ocean   pond   river

_____   _____

_____   _____

Apply What You Know

Evidence Notebook • How does this map show that most water on Earth is salt water? Use evidence to support your answer. Record it in your Evidence Notebook. Compare your answer with a partner.

Communicating Information
Go to the online handbook for tips.

Liquid or Solid

Explore online. ▶

Look at the pictures to explore how bodies of water can be liquid or solid.

liquid at 71 °F

solid at 26 °F

In warm places, bodies of water are liquid. In cold places, ponds, rivers, and lakes may freeze if the temperature is low enough. Fresh water freezes at 32 degrees Fahrenheit (32 °F). Ocean water freezes at about 28 °F. An ocean will never freeze completely. It is too big and salty, and it moves too much. These features are patterns because they show what oceans have in common.

Do the Math! • You can use symbols to compare temperatures of a warm ocean and a cold ocean. Compare the numbers. Write >, <, or =.

71 °F ◯ 26 °F

Use Symbols
Go to the online handbook for tips.

Explore online. ▶

Look at the pictures to explore a lake in the summer and in the winter.

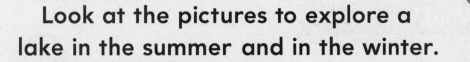

summer   winter

Temperatures are warmer in summer and cooler in winter. This is a pattern. Sometimes it gets cold enough that water freezes.

Patterns • Evaluating Information Go to the online handbook for tips.

Write **liquid** or **solid** to classify each body of water.

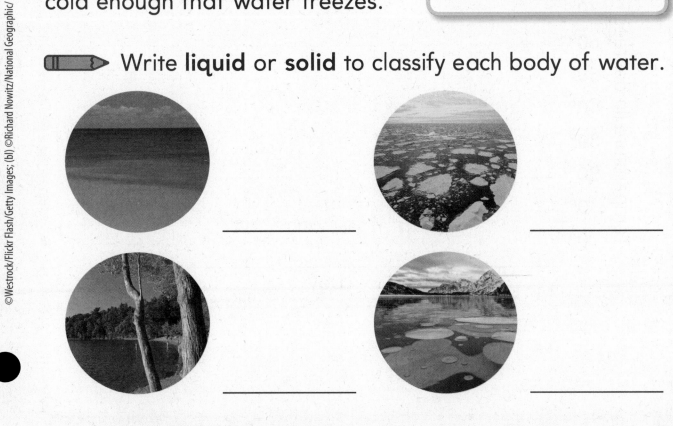

_____   _____

_____   _____

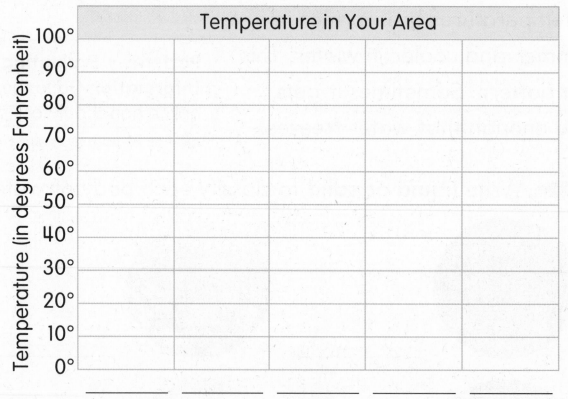

✋ **Apply What You Know**

Does the temperature stay the same from day to day? Use a thermometer to measure temperature at the same time each day for one week. Use your data to complete the graph. Would fresh or salt water freeze at these temperatures? As a class, discuss patterns you see.

💡 **Display Data**
Go to the online handbook for tips.

Temperature in Your Area

Temperature (in degrees Fahrenheit)

100°
90°
80°
70°
60°
50°
40°
30°
20°
10°
0°

Day

Name _____

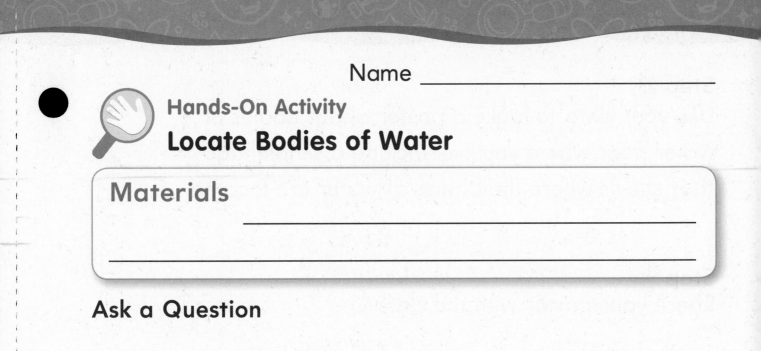

Hands-On Activity
Locate Bodies of Water

Materials

_____

_____

Ask a Question

_____

Test and Record Data Explore online. ▶

Step **1**
Make a plan to research bodies of water where you live.

_____

_____

_____

Step **2**
Record your data.

Bodies of Water	Characteristics

© Houghton Mifflin Harcourt

Step 3

Use your data to make a poster about bodies of water near where you live. Include a simple map that shows where the bodies of water are located.

Step 4

Share your poster with the class.

Make a claim that answers your question.

_____

_____

_____

_____

What is your evidence?

_____

_____

_____

_____

Take It Further

People in Science & Engineering •
John G. Ferris

Explore more online.

• How Can We Conserve Earth's Water?

Explore online. ▶

John G. Ferris was a scientist. He worked hard to take care of groundwater. Groundwater is water under Earth's surface between pieces of soil and rock. Groundwater is important. People drink it. People also use it to water crops. Ferris studied problems with groundwater, such as how to store it and how to keep it clean. He taught people how to care for groundwater.

© Houghton Mifflin Harcourt

Exploring Groundwater

Water on Earth moves from Earth into the air and back again. This movement is called the water cycle. This cycle includes groundwater.

Recall Information
Go to the online handbook for tips.

Explore online. ▶

The sun heats the water and turns it to a vapor. Water vapor rises into the sky and becomes water droplets.

The water droplets form clouds. When the droplets become too heavy, it rains.

Rain falls from clouds onto Earth's surface.

The water flows into bodies of water and becomes surface water. The water cycle starts again.

Much of the rainwater seeps into the soil and becomes groundwater.

Read, Write, Share! • How has Dr. Ferris's work with groundwater helped make our lives better?

Lesson Check

Name _____

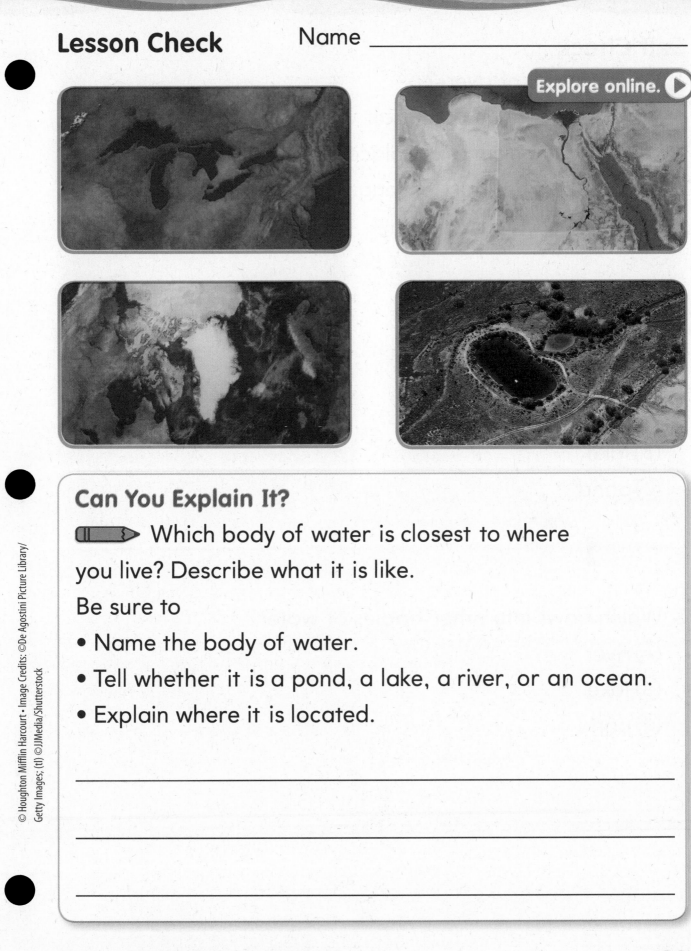

Explore online. ▶

Can You Explain It?

✏️ Which body of water is closest to where you live? Describe what it is like.

Be sure to

• Name the body of water.

• Tell whether it is a pond, a lake, a river, or an ocean.

• Explain where it is located.

_____

_____

_____

Self Check

1. Which is true of rivers?

   Ⓐ They are made up of salt water.

   Ⓑ They flow from a low place to a high place.

   Ⓒ They can be short or long. They can be narrow or wide.

2. Which has land all around it? Choose all correct answers.

   Ⓐ ocean

   Ⓑ lake

   Ⓒ pond

3. Which flows into other bodies of water?

   Ⓐ river

   Ⓑ lake

   Ⓒ pond

4. Which is true of oceans?
   - Ⓐ They flow into rivers.
   - Ⓑ They are smaller than lakes.
   - Ⓒ They are made up of salt water.

5. Write **solid** or **liquid** to describe each body of water.

_____   _____   _____

6. What happens to a lake when it is very cold outside?
   - Ⓐ Ice changes to liquid water.
   - Ⓑ Liquid water changes to ice.
   - Ⓒ Liquid water stays the same.

Engineer It • How Can We Map Land and Water?

This is a three-dimensional map.

By the End of This Lesson

I will be able to find locations using a map. I will be able to make a map.

Why We Use Maps

Look at this picture to explore a map.

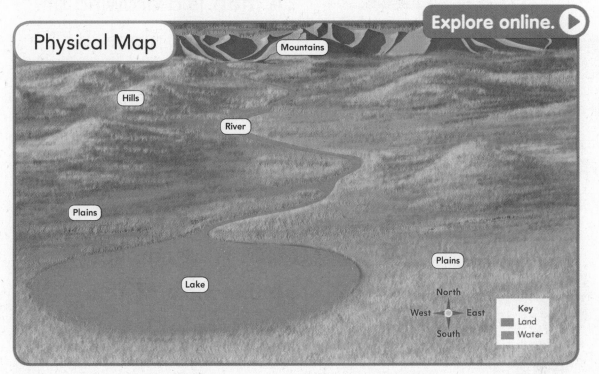

Explore online. ▶

Physical Map

Mountains

Hills

River

Plains

Lake

Plains

North
West ← → East
South

Key
Land
Water

Can you find the land on this map? Can you find the water?

Can You Explain It?

▭▭▭▭▶ What can you find out by exploring a map?

_____

_____

What Is a Map?

Look at these maps to explore the locations of different types of land and bodies of water.

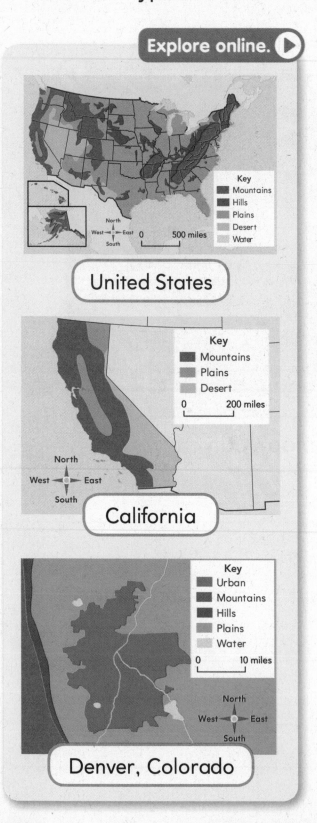

Explore online.

United States

Key
- Mountains
- Hills
- Plains
- Desert
- Water

North West East South
0   500 miles

California

Key
- Mountains
- Plains
- Desert

0   200 miles

North West East South

Denver, Colorado

Key
- Urban
- Mountains
- Hills
- Plains
- Water

0   10 miles

North West East South

A **map** is a drawing or a model of a place. It also shows the distance between two places. Some maps show the shapes of land and bodies of water in a location.

✏️ **How can you use this map of the United States?**

_____

_____

_____

_____

_____

_____

Explore the parts of this map. Underline the sentence that tells what a map key shows. Circle the sentence that tells what a compass rose shows.

A **compass rose** shows directions north, south, east, and west.

A **map title** tells what the map shows.

Explore online.

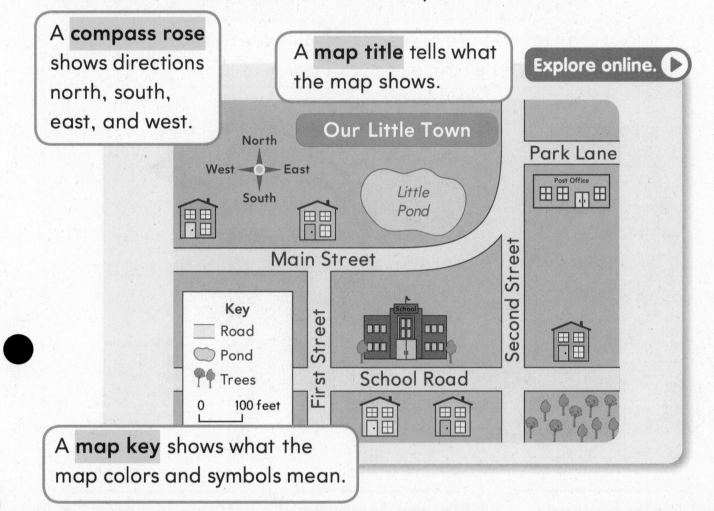

Our Little Town

North
West — East
South

Little Pond

Park Lane

Post Office

Main Street

Second Street

First Street

Key
Road
Pond
Trees
0   100 feet

School

School Road

A **map key** shows what the map colors and symbols mean.

Apply What You Know

Evidence Notebook • With a small group, discuss why a map needs to have a compass rose. Use evidence to support your answer. Record it in your Evidence Notebook.

Patterns • Developing and Using Models
Go to the online handbook for tips.

Use a Map Key

Explore online. ▶

Look at this map to explore a map key.

Deserts are areas with little rain.

Hills are raised areas of land.

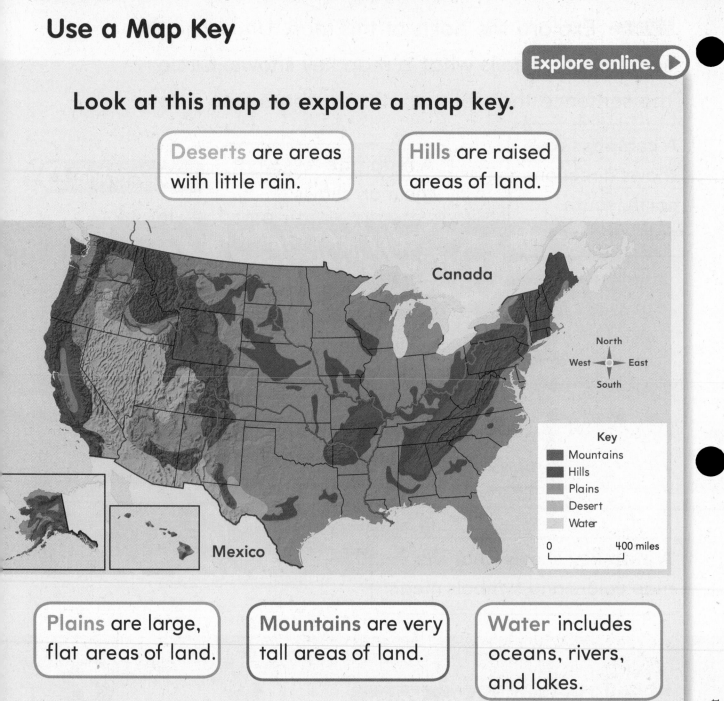

Plains are large, flat areas of land.

Mountains are very tall areas of land.

Water includes oceans, rivers, and lakes.

Each color on a map key stands for a type of land. On the map, these colors show where each type of land is located. The map also shows where water can be found.

Which type of land covers most of the United States?

Ⓐ mountains

Ⓑ plains

Ⓒ deserts

 Where is your state on the map of the United States? Locate it and record its name below.

_____

_____

 What types of land and bodies of water are located in your state?

_____

_____

_____

_____

_____

_____

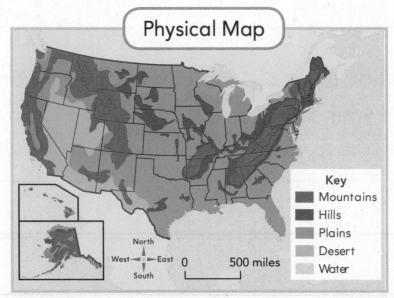

Apply What You Know

Evidence Notebook • How are these maps alike? How are they different? What patterns do you see? Work with a partner to answer these questions. Use evidence to support your answers. Record them in your Evidence Notebook.

Patterns
Go to the online handbook for tips.

Physical Map

Key
- Mountains
- Hills
- Plains
- Desert
- Water

North
West — East
South

0   500 miles

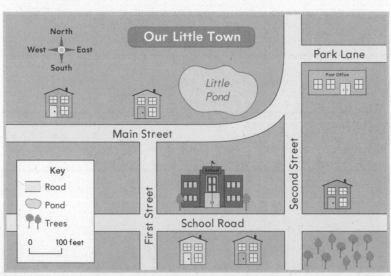

Our Little Town

North
West — East
South

Park Lane

Post Office

Little Pond

Main Street

Second Street

School

Key
- Road
- Pond
- Trees

0   100 feet

First Street

School Road

Name _____

Hands-On Activity

Engineer It • Make a Map

Materials _____

_____

Ask a Question

_____

Test and Record Data

Step 1

Make a plan for your map.
Record ideas and observations
about your map's location.

_____

_____

Step 2

Make your map.
Be sure to include

• a title

• a key

• a compass rose

Step 3
Describe your map and how you made it.

_____

_____

_____

Step 4
Compare your map with the maps of your classmates. Identify patterns.

Make a claim that answers your question.

_____

_____

_____

What is your evidence?

_____

_____

_____

Take It Further

Careers in Science & Engineering • Mapmakers

Explore more online.
• Use a Map Scale

Explore online. ▶

Mapmakers make maps and keep them up to date. They begin by collecting information about a location from other maps and from pictures taken from space. Then, mapmakers use tools such as computers, measurement tools, and the Global Positioning System (GPS) to make different maps.

Read, Write, Share! • Find Out More About Mapmakers

Do research to answer these questions.
• How do you become a mapmaker?
• What types of maps are made?
• What tools do mapmakers use?
• Would you like to be a mapmaker? Explain.

Gather Information
Go to the online handbook for tips.

Do the Math! • Mapmakers must show distances on a map correctly. They must figure out a scale for each map. A map scale shows the relationship between the distance shown on a map and the actual distance it stands for.

Read Numbers
Go to the online handbook for tips.

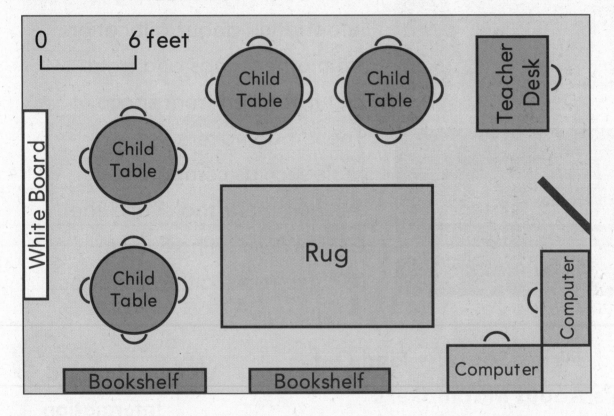

The scale on this classroom map is 1 inch = 6 feet.

The classroom is 36 feet long.

Use a 12-inch ruler to measure the map.

How long is the classroom on the map? ___ inches.

Write an addition sentence to model how the map's measurement relates to the length of the room.

___ + ___ + ___ + ___ + ___ + ___ = 36 feet

Lesson Check

Name _____

Explore online. ▶

Physical Map

Mountains

Hills

River

Plains

Plains

Lake

North
West ◆ East
South

Key
Land
Water

Can You Explain It?

✏️➡ What can you find out by exploring a map?

Be sure to

• Explain how to locate types of land and bodies of water on a map.

• Tell how to find directions.

_____

_____

_____

_____

Self Check

1. What is a compass rose?

    Ⓐ part of a map that tells direction

    Ⓑ part of a map that tells what the map is about

    Ⓒ part of a map that tells what each color or symbol on the map means

2. What does the key on a map show you?

    Ⓐ the title

    Ⓑ the directions

    Ⓒ the meaning of each color or symbol

3. A teacher wants to make a map of her classroom. What should she include? Choose all correct answers.

    Ⓐ a title

    Ⓑ a compass rose

    Ⓒ a key with colors or symbols

4. Which parts of the map show mountains? Circle them.

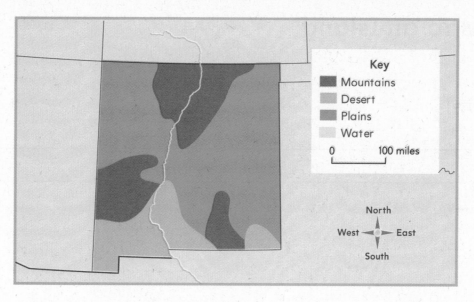

Key
- Mountains
- Desert
- Plains
- Water

0 ___ 100 miles

North
West ← → East
South

5. Which are shown on the map? Choose all correct answers.

Ⓐ desert
Ⓑ plains
Ⓒ water

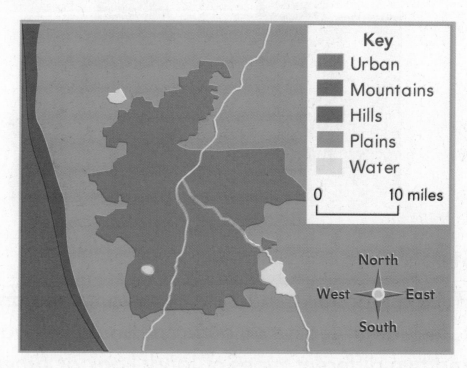

Key
- Urban
- Mountains
- Hills
- Plains
- Water

0 ___ 10 miles

North
West ← → East
South

Unit 4 Performance Task
Map an Island

Materials

_____

_____

STEPS

Step 1

Look at maps of different islands. What pattern do you notice about islands? What does this tell you about the island you will draw?

Step 2

Make a plan for a map of your island and draw it. Include at least two different bodies of water and two different types of land. Look at other maps for ideas.

Step 3

Draw your map. Use colors and symbols to show the different bodies of water and land.

Step 4

Give your map a title. Add a compass rose and a map key to your map so others can read and understand it.

Step 5

Share your map with classmates, and describe your island. Compare maps, and look for patterns.

 Check

_____ I planned and drew a map of an island.

_____ I included two different bodies of water and two kinds of land.

_____ I included a title, a compass rose, and a map key.

_____ I compared my map to the maps of others.

Unit 4 Review

Name _____

1. You see a body of water with land on two sides and flowing water. Which body of water is it?
   - Ⓐ a lake
   - Ⓑ a pond
   - Ⓒ a river

2. Which are **true** of ponds? Choose all correct answers.
   - Ⓐ They are surrounded by land.
   - Ⓑ They contain fresh water.
   - Ⓒ They are bigger than lakes.

3. Why did this pond freeze?
   - Ⓐ The temperature fell below 32 °F.
   - Ⓑ The temperature went above 32 °F.
   - Ⓒ It is winter, and all ponds freeze in winter.

4. Which is **true** of Earth's water? Choose all correct answers.
   - Ⓐ Most of Earth's water is salt water.
   - Ⓑ Most of Earth's water is fresh water.
   - Ⓒ Most of Earth's water is in oceans.

5. Why won't an ocean freeze completely?
   Choose all correct answers.
   Ⓐ It is too big.
   Ⓑ It is too salty.
   Ⓒ It moves too much.

6. What are the different parts of a map? Draw a
   line to match each map part with the words that
   describe it.

title
key
compass rose

shows directions
tells what map colors and symbols mean
names the place the map shows

7. Look at the map of New Mexico.
   What types of land does New Mexico have?
   Choose all correct answers.
   Ⓐ desert
   Ⓑ mountains
   Ⓒ plains

Key
■ Mountains
■ Desert
■ Plains
■ Water

0   100 miles

North
West — East
South

8. What can a map show?
   Choose all correct answers.
   Ⓐ different types of land and water
   Ⓑ the distance between two places
   Ⓒ the time it takes to get to a place

9. Fay looks at a map that has a map scale with 1 inch = 10 miles. She measures 2 inches between her town and the next town. Which number sentence shows how many miles it is to the next town?
   Ⓐ 10 + 10 = 20 miles
   Ⓑ 10 + 2 = 12 miles
   Ⓒ 10 − 2 = 8 miles

10. Layla is at Little Pond. In what direction should she walk to get to the school?
    Ⓐ north
    Ⓑ south
    Ⓒ west

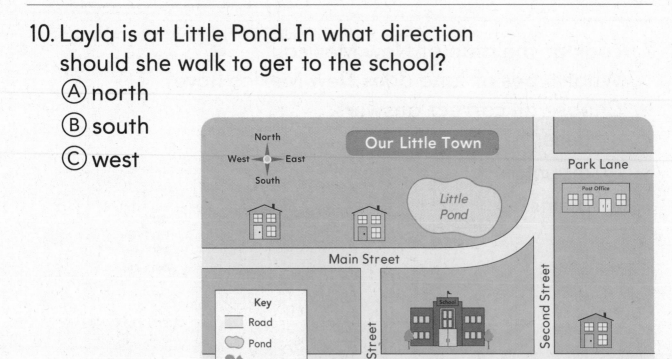

Unit 5
Changes to Earth's Surface

© Houghton Mifflin Harcourt • © Henrik Johansson/Getty Images

Unit Project • Make a Windbreak

How can you stop wind from changing the land? Investigate to find out.

Unit 5 At a Glance

Unit Vocabulary

weathering a process that breaks rock into smaller pieces (p. 226)

erosion the process of picking up and moving rocks, soil, and sand from one place to another (p. 232)

earthquake a sudden shaking of the ground (p. 246)

volcano an opening where lava erupts (p. 248)

landslide the sliding of soil down a slope (p. 250)

hurricane a storm with rain and strong winds (p. 253)

flood water that overflows or soaks an area (p. 255)

windbreak a row of trees used to block wind (p. 270)

dike a wall by a body of water (p.271)

Vocabulary Game • Make a Match

Materials
- 1 set of word cards
- 1 set of definition cards

How to Play
1. Make word and definition cards.
2. Place the cards face down on the table.
3. Pick a word card and a definition card.
4. If you make a match, keep the cards.
5. If not, put the cards back.

Nature slowly changes rocks on Earth.

By the End of This Lesson

I will be able to describe some changes that happen slowly on Earth.

Slow Changes to Earth's Surface

Look at these pictures to explore how Bryce Canyon has formed over time.

Explore online.

Can You Explain It?

 What causes slow changes to rocks on Earth?

_____

_____

_____

_____

Weathering by Wind

Look at these pictures to explore how weathering causes slow changes to Earth over time.

Explore online. ▶

4 million years ago | Today

before | after

Weathering is a process that breaks rocks into smaller pieces. Wind and water smash against these mountains every day. Bits of rock break off very slowly. Over millions of years, the mountains become smoother and more rounded.

Explore online. ▶

Weathering by wind is a slow change. Wind carries bits of sand. The sand hits the rock when the wind blows. Over time, the rock becomes weaker. Small pieces break off. Over many years, weathering from wind changes the shape of the rock.

How will wind change a rock?

Ⓐ Wind will blow a rock to a new place.

Ⓑ Wind will turn a rock into a mountain.

Ⓒ Wind will weather a rock.

 Apply What You Know

Evidence Notebook • Observe a rock. Record your observations. Then rub sandpaper all over the rock for 5 minutes. Observe the rock again. Did it change? How does this relate to weathering? Use evidence to support your answer. Record it in your Evidence Notebook.

Constructing Explanations and Designing Solutions
Go to the online handbook for tips.

Weathering by Water and Ice

Look at the pictures to explore how water and ice cause slow changes to Earth's surface.

Explore online. ▶

Water and ice can break down rocks into smaller pieces. Most rocks have small cracks. When it rains, water gets into these cracks. Some water stays in the cracks.

In winter, the water in the cracks turns to ice. Ice takes up more space than water. This causes the ice to push against the cracks and make them bigger.

In spring, the ice melts. The cracks are bigger now. This cycle repeats every year. After many years, these cracks are big enough to cause the rock to break into pieces.

Which actions repeat in the process of weathering by water and ice? Choose all correct answers.

Stability and Change
Go to the online handbook for tips.

Ⓐ Water gets into cracks in rocks.

Ⓑ Water freezes to form ice in the cracks and pushes against them.

Ⓒ Wind blows water to a new place.

Apply What You Know

Constructing Explanations and Designing Solutions Go to the online handbook for tips.

Evidence Notebook • Work with a partner. Fill one-half of a small plastic cup with water. Mark the water line. Put the cup in a freezer overnight. Observe the cup and the mark the next day. Do you observe any changes? How does this relate to weathering? Use evidence to support your answer. Record it in your Evidence Notebook.

© Houghton Mifflin Harcourt

Weathering by Plants

Look at the pictures to explore how plant roots cause changes to Earth's surface.

Explore online.

Plant roots grow into cracks in rock and press on it.

This plant grew through rock. As its roots and trunk grew, the pressure was too much for the rock. The rock split in half.

Look at the roots. Nearby are pebbles and soil. Over a long time, these roots have split the rock so many times that it became pebbles and soil.

How do plants cause changes to Earth's surface by weathering? Write **1**, **2**, and **3** to show the correct order.

Explore online. ▶

_____   _____   _____

Apply What You Know

Evidence Notebook • Have you ever seen weathering by plants? Think about what you have observed. Draw to record your observations in your Evidence Notebook. Share your picture with a classmate. Use evidence to explain how the plants caused changes by weathering to the rock.

Erosion by Wind

Look at the picture to explore how erosion causes slow changes to Earth's surface.

Explore online. ▶

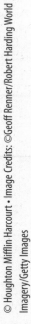

Erosion is the picking up and moving of rocks, soil, or sand from one place to another. Wind, water, and ice can all cause erosion. Erosion happens slowly over long periods of time. Changes from erosion may reshape a beach, a coastline, or a whole island.

Look at these pictures to explore how wind causes erosion.

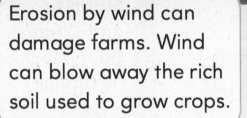

Explore online. ▶

Erosion by wind can damage farms. Wind can blow away the rich soil used to grow crops.

Erosion by wind can reshape deserts. Wind can bury an entire area in dust, sand, or ash.

Erosion by wind moves rocks, soil, and sand from one place to another. This often happens in dry places. There, wind can easily pick up and blow around small, dry pieces of sand or dust. This causes slow changes to Earth's surface.

This picture shows erosion by wind. What is happening in the picture?

Ⓐ The wind moves sand from one place to another.

Ⓑ The wind breaks sand into smaller pieces.

Ⓒ The wind pushes bits of sand together into rocks.

✋ Apply What You Know

Evidence Notebook • Pile sand into a small mountain on a tray. Sketch a picture of it in your Evidence Notebook. Then blow air gently through a straw toward the mountain. Observe what happens. Sketch it in your Evidence Notebook. Use evidence to explain how the mountain changed and how this relates to erosion. Repeat the activity and use different speeds of air.

💡 **Stability and Change**
Go to the online handbook for tips.

Erosion by Water and Ice

Look at these pictures to explore how flowing water carves a canyon over many years.

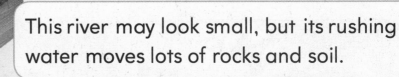Explore online.

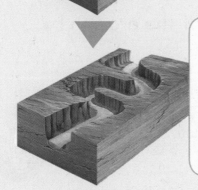

This river may look small, but its rushing water moves lots of rocks and soil.

Over many years, the river has carved away some of the rock. It has carried away bits of rock and soil. It has slowly made the canyon deeper and wider.

The flowing river keeps carrying away bits of rock and soil. This erosion causes the canyon to be deeper and wider. What do you think the canyon will look like a long time from now?

Do the Math! • The Grand Canyon is 277 miles long. Which is another way to write the number 277?

Ⓐ 2 + 7 + 7

Ⓑ 200 + 70 + 7

Ⓒ 270 + 7 + 7

Stability and Change • Understand Place Value Go to the online handbook for tips.

© Houghton Mifflin Harcourt

A glacier is a thick sheet of moving ice. Look at the pictures to explore how a glacier causes Earth's surface to change.

Explore online. ▶

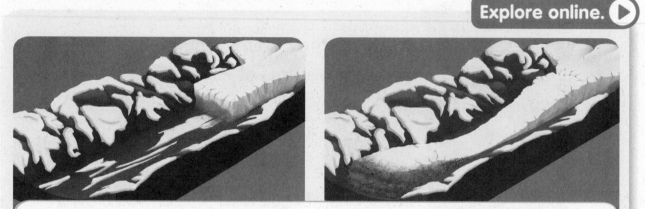

Most glaciers are very large and powerful. They can move gigantic boulders, as well as soil, sand, and rocks. Over many years they travel great distances, taking a lot of soil and rocks with them. Glaciers cause most of the erosion by ice on Earth.

 Apply What You Know

This picture shows a single moment at a beach. However, a beach is always changing. Work with a partner. Talk about how wind and water can change a beach over time. Record your answer.

Stability and Change Go to the online handbook for tips.

Name _____

Model Erosion

Materials _____
_____

Ask a Question

_____

Test and Record Data Explore online. ▶

Step 1

Make a model of a stream. Observe the model before adding water to it. Record your observations.

_____

_____

Step 2

Add water to the model. Observe the model. Record your observations.

Step 3

Analyze your results. Compare the model before and after you added water to it.

Before	After

Step 4

Identify any differences you observed. How do they help you understand how water causes slow changes to Earth's surface?

Make a claim that answers the question.

_____

_____

_____

What is your evidence?

_____

_____

Take It Further
Careers in Science & Engineering •
Farming

Explore more online.
- How Does a Delta Form?

Explore online. ▶

Erosion can be harmful to farmland. If too much soil erodes, farmers cannot grow crops.

Farmers can slow erosion by adding plants. These plants have roots that help keep soil in place when the wind blows.

Another way farmers can slow erosion is by planting trees. The trees break up the gusts of wind. This keeps soil in place, too.

Read, Write, Share! • Find out more about how farmers use plants to slow erosion. Do research using online and print resources. Record what you find out. Be sure to include a main idea and details. Share your findings with your classmates.

Describe Details • Gather Information
Go to the online handbook for tips.

_____

_____

_____

_____

Do you still have questions about how farmers help Earth's surface? Ask a farmer. Write a friendly letter to a local farmer. Introduce yourself. Describe what you are learning in school. Then ask your questions about erosion and what farmers can do to help slow it.

Ask Questions
Go to the online handbook for tips.

Lesson Check

Name _____

Explore online. ▶

Can You Explain It?

✏️ What causes slow changes to rocks on Earth?
Be sure to

• Explain changes caused by weathering.

• Explain changes caused by erosion.

• Describe whether these changes happened slowly or quickly.

_____

_____

_____

_____

_____

_____

Self Check

1. Which process do these pictures show?

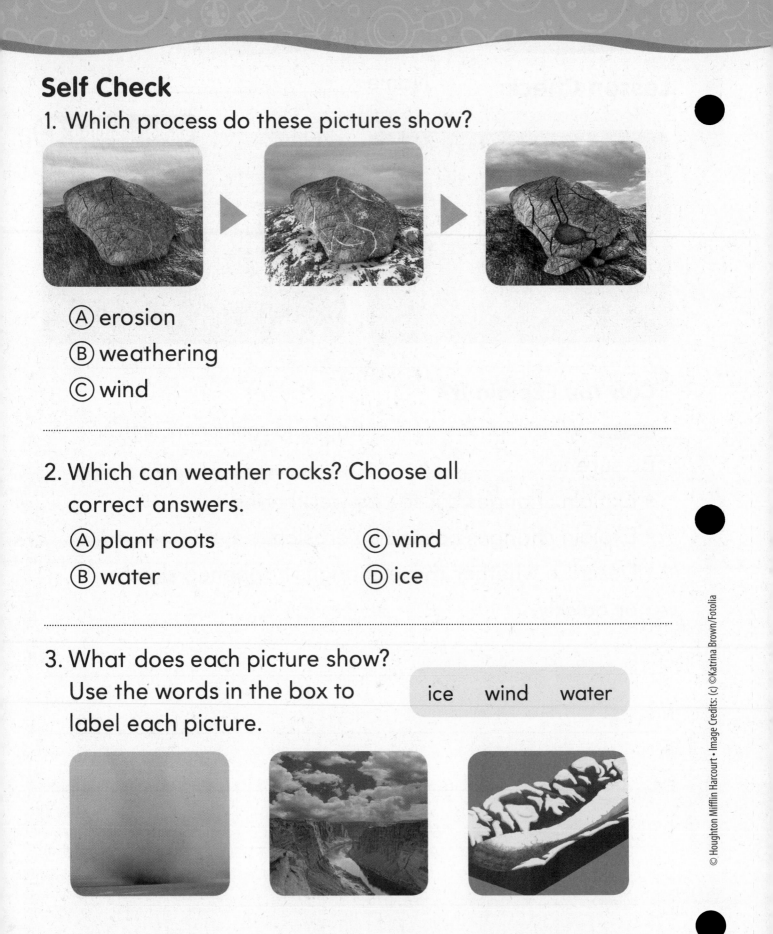

Ⓐ erosion

Ⓑ weathering

Ⓒ wind

2. Which can weather rocks? Choose all correct answers.

Ⓐ plant roots   Ⓒ wind

Ⓑ water   Ⓓ ice

3. What does each picture show? Use the words in the box to label each picture.

ice   wind   water

_____   _____   _____

4. How does erosion form a canyon? Write **1**, **2**, and **3** to show the correct order.

_____ _____ _____

5. How do glaciers cause Earth's surface to change?

Ⓐ They move boulders.

Ⓑ They move sand.

Ⓒ They move soil.

Some changes on Earth happen quickly.

By the End of This Lesson

I will be able to describe changes to Earth that happen quickly.

Quick Changes to Earth's Surface

Look at the pictures to explore how a volcanic eruption caused the land to change.

Explore online. ▶

Can You Explain It?

✏️ How can a volcano cause Earth's surface to change quickly?

_____

_____

_____

_____

Earthquakes

Explore online.

before

after

An earthquake happens quickly. The shaking starts suddenly. It usually lasts for only a few seconds.

An earthquake may cause many changes to the land. Cracks may form on Earth's surface. The ground may shift and lose some strength. When the ground shakes, everything on it shakes, too. Buildings may sway. Trees may fall over.

An **earthquake** is a sudden shaking of the ground that causes land to rise and fall. It can cause fast changes to Earth's surface.

Which changes may be caused by an earthquake? Choose all correct answers.

Ⓐ cracks on Earth's surface

Ⓑ shifting ground

Ⓒ swaying buildings

Apply What You Know

Evidence Notebook • Model Earth's surface during an earthquake. Observe what happens.

Step 1: Break a graham cracker in half.

Step 2: Put the two pieces back together so they touch.

Step 3: Move one piece away from you while moving the other piece towards you. Repeat two times.

Step 4: Observe what happens to the crackers. Record your observations in your Evidence Notebook. Use evidence to describe how it is similar to what happens to Earth's surface during an earthquake.

Stability and Change • **Constructing Explanations**
Go to the online handbook for tips.

Volcanoes

Explore online.

Before many volcanoes erupt, they look like quiet mountains. This is Mount St. Helens just days before it erupted in 1980.

During an eruption, ash and dust burst from the opening at the top. Lava pours out from openings in the mountain. All of this happens quickly.

After the eruption, a huge chunk has blown off the mountaintop. Ash and dust cover the ground nearby. Some volcanoes gain new land at the bottom where lava cools into rock.

A **volcano** is an opening in Earth's surface where lava, gases, and bits of rock erupt. It can cause fast changes.

248

Do the Math! • Zukur Volcano is 2047 feet tall. Masaya Volcano is 2083 feet tall. Write <, >, or = to compare their heights.

2047 feet ◯ 2083 feet

Use Symbols
Go to the online handbook for tips.

 Apply What You Know

 Draw before and after pictures of a volcano changing Earth's surface. Share your drawing with a classmate. Use evidence to explain the changes.

© Houghton Mifflin Harcourt

Landslides

A **landslide** is when rocks and soil slide down a hill, mountain, or other slope. Once a landslide starts, it moves fast. The rushing soil, rocks, and mud can run down a slope at 10 to 35 miles per hour. Look at the pictures to explore how a landslide changes Earth's surface quickly.

Explore online.

before

A landslide starts when the soil and rocks on the side of a slope become too heavy and start to slide. Often, heavy rain triggers a landslide.

after

A landslide moves a lot of land very quickly. Both the slope and the area around it change shape. Large areas can be buried or washed out.

© Houghton Mifflin Harcourt • Image Credits: (cl) ©International Photobank/Alamy; (tr) ©Medford Taylor/Getty Images; (bl) ©Mike Kipling Photography/Alamy

● What changes do landslides make to Earth's surface? Choose all correct answers.

Ⓐ They start volcanoes and earthquakes.

Ⓑ They change the shape of hills.

Ⓒ They bury or wash out areas around a slope.

 Apply What You Know

✏️➤ Draw a picture of how a landslide causes changes to Earth's surface. Use evidence to describe the changes.

Constructing Explanations
Go to the online handbook for tips.

Look at the pictures of three types of fast changes to Earth. Draw a line to match each picture to the change it describes.

Stability and Change
Go to the online handbook for tips.

Explore online.

Rocks and soil rush down a slope.

The ground shakes.

Lava, gas, and rocks erupt.

Hurricanes

Explore online. ▶

The beach looks quiet now, but a hurricane is on the way. Hurricanes form over warm water in the ocean.

The storm brings strong wind and heavy rain. The wind makes large, powerful waves that crash on the beach.

Wind, waves, and rain move sand to new places. A hurricane can uproot trees and cause flooding, too.

A **hurricane** is a tropical storm with powerful winds and heavy rain. It can cause fast changes to Earth's surface.

© Houghton Mifflin Harcourt • Image Credits: (t) ©James P. Blair/Getty Images; (d) ©Steven D Starr/Corbis Historical/Getty Images; (b) ©Mike Slater/Alamy

Lesson 2 • What Changes on Earth Happen Quickly?

✏️ What does the picture show? Write to describe what you see.

_____

_____

_____

_____

_____

Apply What You Know

Evidence Notebook • Think about the changes that a hurricane causes to Earth's surface. Which two events does a hurricane bring? How do they cause Earth's surface to change? Record your answers in your Evidence Notebook. Use evidence to explain how they cause changes.

Stability and Change
Go to the online handbook for tips.

Floods

Look at the picture to explore how a flood changes Earth's surface.

Explore online. ▶

A **flood** occurs when a huge amount of water overflows or soaks an area that is usually dry. A flood starts quickly, often with little warning. Rain may fill a river with extra water. When the river cannot hold any more, it overflows. That triggers a flood. A flood can knock down trees and wash away land. It can bury huge areas with mud or silt. When the water goes down, the land is changed.

✏️ What takes place during a flood? Write **1**, **2**, and **3** to show the correct order

_____   _____   _____

✋ **Apply What You Know**

Read, Write, Share! • Work with a partner. First, state a claim: Floods cause quick changes to Earth's surface. Next, gather information to use as evidence to support your claim. Look at books and online sources. Then, use the information to write a report. Share your report with your classmates.

💡 **Participate in a Research Project • Use Digital Tools to Publish Writing** Go to the online handbook for tips.

Name _____

Materials _____

Ask a Question

_____

Test and Record Data   Explore online. ▶

Step 1

Make a model of land. Observe the model before adding water. Record your observations.

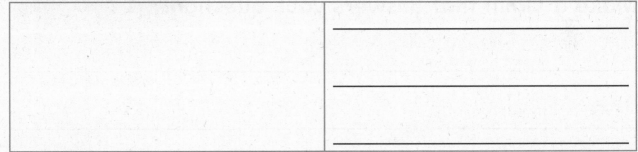

Step 2

Add water to the model. Observe the model. Record your observations.

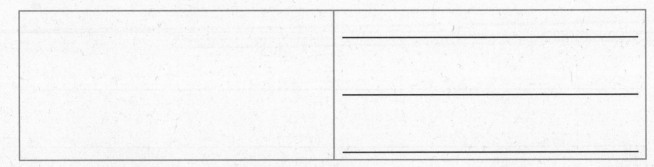

© Houghton Mifflin Harcourt

Step 3

Analyze your results. Compare the model before and after you added water to it. Draw your results.

Before	After

Step 4

What differences do you observe? How do they help you understand how water causes quick changes to Earth's surface?

Make a claim that answers your question.

_____

_____

_____

What is your evidence?

_____

_____

_____

Take It Further

People in Science & Engineering •
Dr. Rosaly M.C. Lopes

Explore more online.

• Earthquake Locations

Explore online. ▶

Dr. Rosaly Lopes is a volcanologist. A volcanologist is a scientist who studies volcanoes. Dr. Lopes studies volcanoes on Earth and on other planets. How does she do this?

Dr. Lopes visited the Yasur volcano in the South Pacific Ocean.

Some volcanoes leave colorful mineral deposits.

Dr. Lopes takes an Explorers Club flag on many of her trips.

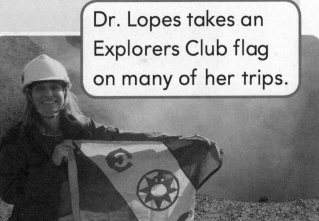

First, Dr. Lopes studies volcanoes on Earth. She explores volcanoes that explode like fireworks and flow like rivers. She also explores volcanoes with lava lakes. She measures how lava cools at each volcano and looks for patterns.

Then, Dr. Lopes studies images from space. She looks for cooling patterns in these images to locate volcanoes on other planets and moons. Dr. Lopes has used patterns to discover more than 70 volcanoes on Io, which is one of Jupiter's moons. These patterns tell her that Io has many lava lakes. Dr. Lopes believes that Io must be very colorful due to the number of deposits from volcanoes.

How does Dr. Lopes study volcanoes?
Choose all correct answers.

Ⓐ She explores different volcanoes.

Ⓑ She measures how lava cools.

Ⓒ She looks for patterns in images from space.

Name _____

Explore online. ▶

Can You Explain It?

✏️ How can a volcano cause Earth's surface to change quickly?

Be sure to

• Describe the event.

• Explain how it causes changes to Earth's surface.

_____

_____

_____

_____

_____

Self Check

1. How does a hurricane cause changes to Earth's surface? Write **1**, **2**, and **3** to show the correct order.

_____ _____ _____

2. How long does a landslide last?
   Ⓐ a few minutes
   Ⓑ a few months
   Ⓒ a few years

3. What are some effects of a hurricane? Choose all correct answers.
   Ⓐ Beaches are reshaped.
   Ⓑ Farms get buried in ash and dust.
   Ⓒ Trees blow over.

4. Draw a line to match the cause in each picture on the left with its effect on the right.

> Lava can form new land.

> Rocks and mud can wash away trees.

> Wind and water can move sand.

5. What happens when the ground begins to shake?
   (A) earthquake
   (B) flood
   (C) volcano

6. How can you describe floods and hurricanes? Write **flood** or **hurricane** in each sentence.

A _____ happens when waters overflow.

A _____ brings high winds and large

waves to a coastline.

Lesson 3

Engineer It • How Can We Prevent Wind and Water from Changing Land?

A sea wall can protect the shore from ocean waves.

By the End of This Lesson

I will be able to describe and evaluate different solutions to help stop wind and water from changing land.

Preventing Changes to Land

Look at the pictures to explore how heavy rainfall can cause changes to the land.

Explore online. ▶

Can You Solve It?

 What can people do to prevent water and wind from changing the land?

_____

_____

_____

Changes Caused by Wind

Explore online. ▶

Look at these pictures to explore
how erosion by wind can harm the land.

before

after

A farm has rich soil to grow crops. Wind can blow
the soil away. The land is useless to farmers. They
cannot grow crops in soil with no nutrients.

before

after

These pictures show
the same beach. Once,
there were tall sand
dunes. Over time, wind
carried away much of
the sand, making the
dunes smaller.

✏️➤ Underline the sentence that tells what
caused the farm to lose its healthy soil.

Do the Math! • A beach is 52 feet wide. Strong winds cause a lot of the sand to be eroded. The beach now measures 37 feet. How much smaller is the beach now because of wind erosion?

Ⓐ 25 feet

Ⓑ 89 feet

Ⓒ 15 feet

Subtract Lengths
Go to the online handbook for tips.

Apply What You Know

Evidence Notebook • Think about how wind can change the land. Why do you think it is important to stop wind erosion? Write two reasons why. Use evidence to support your answers. Record your answers in your Evidence Notebook.

© Houghton Mifflin Harcourt

Changes Caused by Water

Explore online. ▶

Look at the pictures to explore how water can cause harmful changes to land.

Rushing water can crash into riverbanks. It moves the soil from one place to another. It causes the edges of rivers to change shape.

Heavy rains on a mountain slope can cause a landslide. The wet soil becomes loose and muddy. It slides downhill.

Floods can damage the land. The water rises and covers large areas of land. It can knock over bushes and trees.

✏️ How can water harm the land? Match the pictures with the labels that tell how.

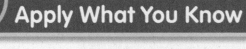
| flood | rushing water | heavy rains |

✋ **Apply What You Know**

Evidence Notebook • Look at the picture. What is happening to the farmland? In your Evidence Notebook, record two ways that flooding harms farmland. Use evidence to support your answer.

Ways to Prevent Changes to Land

Look at the pictures to explore how people try to prevent wind and water from changing the land.

Explore online. ▶

Farmers have ways to keep wind from blowing away rich soil. They plant trees and shrubs to help block the wind. These trees and shrubs are called **windbreaks**.

Beach grass can help keep some of the sand from blowing away. Fences help block some of the wind and keep sand from being moved.

Bags of sand can help prevent or slow flooding. People pour sand into water-resistant bags. Then they stack the sandbags to build a wall. The wall keeps the water from covering the land.

A **dike** is a wall by a river or another body of water. People build dikes in places where the water often rises and falls. Dikes can be made of concrete, wood, clay, or other materials.

Look at the pictures to explore several ways to prevent landslides. Some solutions work better than others.

Constructing Explanations
Go to the online handbook for tips.

Explore online. ▶

Plant roots hold soil in place, but heavy rain can loosen the soil.

A wall keeps mud and rocks in place, but it does not prevent a landslide.

Technology like wires and brackets hold the whole hillside in place.

Apply What You Know

Read, Write, Share! • What are two questions you have about ways to prevent wind and water from changing the land? Look in books, magazines, or on the Internet to find answers. Share your questions and answers with your class.

Ask and Answer Questions
Go to the online handbook for tips.

Hands-On Activity

Engineer It • Prevent Water from Changing Land

Materials _____

_____

Ask a Question

_____

Test and Record Data Explore online.

Step 1

Make a model. Observe the model before adding water. Record your observations and data.

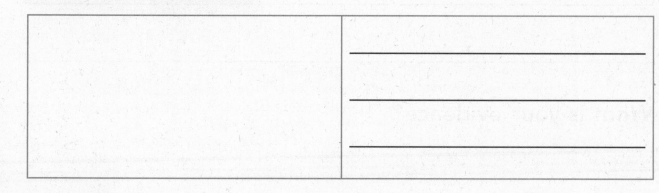

© Houghton Mifflin Harcourt

Step 2

Add water to your model. Observe the model.

Record your observations and data.

Step 3

Design and build a solution to slow or prevent changes by the water. Rebuild the model. Put the design solution in place.

Step 4

Test your design. Fill the model with about the same amount of water as before. Observe your model and measure the height of its banks. Record your observations and data.

Step 5

Revise and retest your design. Compare your results with the results of other groups.

Make a claim that answers your question.

_____

_____

_____

What is your evidence?

_____

_____

_____

Take It Further

Careers in Science & Engineering •
Geotechnical Engineer

Explore more online.
• The Dust Bowl

Explore online. ▶

Geotechnical engineers study soil and rock to plan the best way to build things on land.

They also work to keep wind and water from changing the land. They build dikes to stop flooding. They plan walls to protect the shore. They design technology to stop landslides.

What do geotechnical engineers do?
Choose all correct answers.

Ⓐ They study soil and rock.

Ⓑ They plan the best way to build things on land.

Ⓒ They work to change the land.

What would you design if you were a geotechnical engineer? Design a structure that would reduce damage from wind or water. Then draw and label your design. Explain your idea to a partner or to the class.

Name _____

Explore online.

Can You Solve It?

What can people do to prevent water and wind from changing the land?

Be sure to

- Identify and describe ways to prevent flooding.
- Identify and describe ways to prevent wind erosion.
- Identify and describe ways to prevent landslides.

_____

_____

_____

_____

_____

Self Check

1. Which shows a way to help stop wind from blowing soil from a farm or field?

2. How can people help prevent or slow floods? Choose all correct answers.

3. What do designs to prevent landslides try to do?

Ⓐ slow landslides down

Ⓑ keep landslides from starting

Ⓒ make landslides smaller

4. What change are people trying to prevent in each picture? Use a word from the box to identify the change.

_____

_____

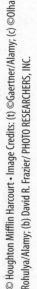

_____

5. Which country would need to build dikes? Choose the best answer.

Ⓐ Mongolia, which is high in the mountains

Ⓑ Netherlands, which is mostly at or below sea level

Ⓒ Chile, which is covered with a sandy desert

Lesson 3 • Engineer It • How Can We Prevent Wind and Water from Changing Land?

Unit 5 Performance Task

Engineer It • Build an Earthquake-Proof Structure

Materials

_____

_____

STEPS

Step 1

Define a Problem You want to build a structure that can survive an earthquake.

Step 2

Plan and Build Think about the materials you will use. Come up with at least two ideas for your structure. Build your structure.

Step 3

Test and Improve Test your design. Shake your structure. Does it stay together? Does it fall apart?

Step 4

Redesign How can you improve your design? Change how you put the materials together to make your structure stronger.

Step 5

Communicate Explain how your structure works. Use evidence to tell how your design solves the problem.

✔ Check

_____ I built a structure that can survive an earthquake.

_____ I tested my structure.

_____ I improved the design of my structure.

_____ I shared my results.

_____ I used evidence to explain how my design solves a problem.

© Houghton Mifflin Harcourt

Name _____

1. How does wind cause weathering to rocks?
   Ⓐ Wind moves rocks.
   Ⓑ Wind makes rocks wet.
   Ⓒ Wind blows sand against rocks.

2. What caused this arch to form over a long period of time?
   Ⓐ a glacier
   Ⓑ a hurricane
   Ⓒ water

3. Each winter, water freezes in the cracks of this rock. How does this ice cause weathering to the rock?
   Ⓐ Ice makes the cracks in the rock bigger each year.
   Ⓑ Ice makes the cracks in the rock thinner each year.
   Ⓒ Ice makes the cracks in the rock darker each year.

4. Which can cause erosion? Choose all correct answers.
   Ⓐ Wood can cause erosion.
   Ⓑ Wind can cause erosion.
   Ⓒ Water can cause erosion.

5. Which changes Earth's surface quickly? Choose all correct answers.
   Ⓐ flood
   Ⓑ volcano
   Ⓒ weathering

6. What is one effect of a volcano?
   Ⓐ It causes a hurricane.
   Ⓑ It floods the land with water.
   Ⓒ It covers the ground nearby with ash and dust.

7. A farmer planted a row of trees at the end of a field. What does this farmer hope to prevent?
   Ⓐ water from flooding the field
   Ⓑ wind from blowing away soil
   Ⓒ lava from covering the field

8. Which items can you use to build something that will slow or stop a flood? Choose all correct answers.

Ⓐ empty sandbag   Ⓑ concrete cinder block   Ⓒ pile of builder's sand

9. Look at this wall built on the side of a mountain. What do the people who built it hope to prevent?

Ⓐ a flood

Ⓑ a landslide

Ⓒ a hurricane

10. Li-Mei is building a structure to protect a town from floods. The town has an existing structure that is 5 feet tall. But in the past, floodwaters rose 3 feet higher than that. How high should the new structure be?

Ⓐ at least 3 feet

Ⓑ at least 5 feet

Ⓒ at least 8 feet

Interactive Glossary

This Interactive Glossary will help you learn how to spell and define a vocabulary term. The Glossary will give you the meaning of the term. It will also show you a picture to help you understand what the term means.

Where you see ▱▱▱▱▱⬢, write your own words or draw your own picture to help you remember what the term means.

Glossary Pronunciation Key

With every glossary term, there is also a phonetic respelling. A phonetic respelling writes the word the way it sounds, which can help you pronounce new or unfamiliar words. Use this key to help you understand the respellings.

Sound	As in	Phonetic Respelling	Sound	As in	Phonetic Respelling
a	bat	(BAT)	oh	over	(OH•ver)
ah	lock	(LAHK)	oo	pool	(POOL)
air	rare	(RAIR)	ow	out	(OWT)
ar	argue	(AR•gyoo)	oy	foil	(FOYL)
aw	law	(LAW)	s	cell	(SEL)
ay	face	(FAYS)		sit	(SIT)
ch	chapel	(CHAP•uhl)	sh	sheep	(SHEEP)
e	test	(TEST)	th	that	(THAT)
	metric	(MEH•trik)		thin	(THIN)
ee	eat	(EET)	u	pull	(PUL)
	feet	(FEET)	uh	medal	(MED•uhl)
	ski	(SKEE)		talent	(TAL•uhnt)
er	paper	(PAY•per)		pencil	(PEN•suhl)
	fern	(FERN)		onion	(UHN•yuhn)
eye	idea	(eye•DEE•uh)		playful	(PLAY•fuhl)
i	bit	(BIT)		dull	(DUHL)
ing	going	(GOH•ing)	y	yes	(YES)
k	card	(KARD)		ripe	(RYP)
	kite	(KYT)	z	bags	(BAGZ)
ngk	bank	(BANGK)	zh	treasure	(TREZH•er)

Interactive Glossary

compass rose (KUM·puhs ROHZ)

A part of a map that shows directions north, south, east, and west. (p. 205)

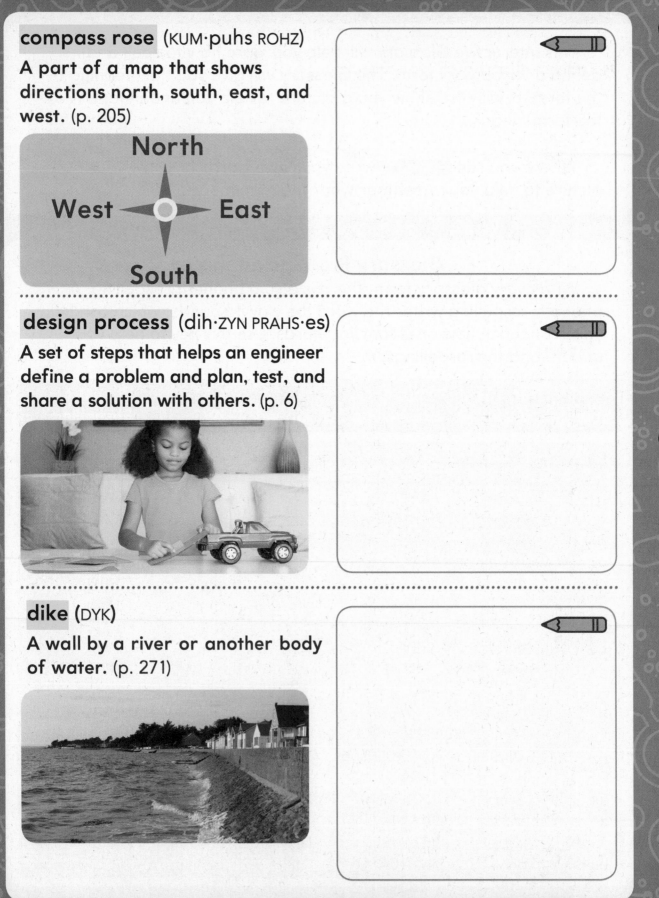

design process (dih·ZYN PRAHS·es)

A set of steps that helps an engineer define a problem and plan, test, and share a solution with others. (p. 6)

dike (DYK)

A wall by a river or another body of water. (p. 271)

earthquake (ERTH·kwayk)

A sudden shaking of the ground that causes land to rise and fall. (p. 246)

engineer (en·juh·NEER)

A person who uses math and science to define and solve problems. (p. 6)

erosion (uh·ROH·zhuhn)

The process of picking up and moving rocks, soil, or sand from one place to another. (p. 232)

Interactive Glossary

flood (FLUD)

A huge amount of water overflowing or soaking an area that is usually dry. (p. 255)

freeze (FREEZ)

A change that happens by removing heat, which causes a liquid to become a solid. (p. 80)

habitat (HAB·ih·tat)

A place where living things get the food, water, air, and shelter needed to live. (p. 142, 158)

hurricane (HER·ih·kayn)

A tropical storm with powerful winds and heavy rain. (p. 253)

irreversible (ir·i·VER·suh·buhl)

A change that cannot be reversed, or undone. (p. 93)

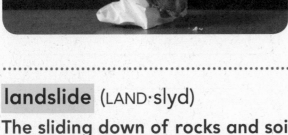

landslide (LAND·slyd)

The sliding down of rocks and soil on or from a hill, mountain, or other slope. (p. 250)

Interactive Glossary

liquid (LIK·wid)

A state of matter that takes the shape of its container. (p. 49)

map (MAP)

A drawing or model of a place. (p. 204)

Horseshoe
Meadowlark Drive
North
West — East
South
Goldfinch Road
First Street
Second Street
Third Street
Fourth Street
Key
Road

map key (MAP KEE)

A part of a map that shows what the map colors and symbols mean. (p. 205)

Key
Road
Lake
Trees
0 100 feet

map title (MAP TYT·uhl)

A part of a map that tells what the map shows. (p. 205)

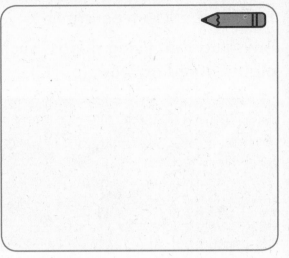

matter (MAT·er)

Anything that takes up space. (p. 44)

melt (MELT)

A change that happens by adding heat, which causes a solid to become a liquid. (p. 74)

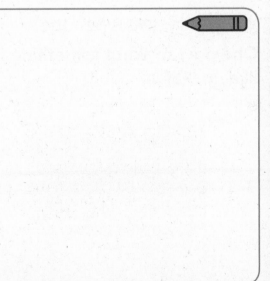

Interactive Glossary

nutrient (NOO·tree·uhnt)

Anything that living things, such as plants, need as food. (p. 112)

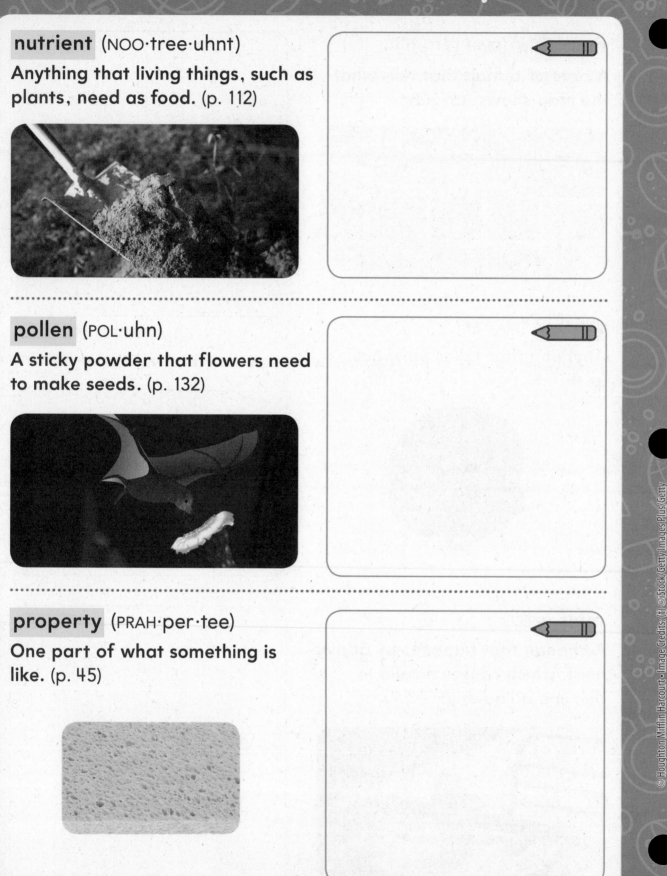

pollen (POL·uhn)

A sticky powder that flowers need to make seeds. (p. 132)

property (PRAH·per·tee)

One part of what something is like. (p. 45)

reversible (ree·VER·suh·buhl)

A change that can be reversed, or undone. (p. 90)

---

solid (SAHL·id)

A state of matter that keeps its shape. (p. 48)

---

solution (suh·LOO·shuhn)

An answer to a problem. (p. 6)

Interactive Glossary

strength (STRENGTH)

A good feature. (p. 24)

volcano (vahl·KAY·noh)

An opening in Earth's surface where lava, gases, and bits of rock erupt. (p. 248)

weakness (WEEK·nis)

A flawed feature. (p. 24)

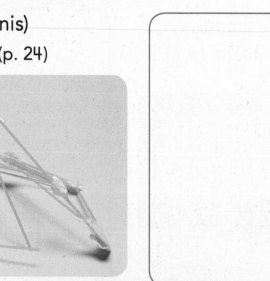

weathering (WEH·ther·ing)

A process that breaks rock into smaller pieces. (p. 226)

windbreak (WIND·brayk)

A row of trees or shrubs planted to help block the wind. (p. 270)

Index

Index

Index

Index

in design process, 8, 11, 32, 33, 68
erosion, 237–238
of a flood, 257–258
habitats, 149–150
mechanical engineering, 15
preventing water from changing land, 273–274
quick changes on Earth, 257–258
tool, 129–131
mongoose, 167
mountains
  landslides, 250, 268
  on a map, 206
  volcanoes, 248
  weathering, 226, 234

N

North America, climate types in, 119–120
nutrients, plants needing, 112, 114

O

objects. *See also* **matter**
  breaking down, 62
  building up new, 62

built from small pieces, 62–63, 65–67
identifying similarities in, 64
made up of smaller pieces, 60–70
putting together, 61
ramps helping to move, 5, 8
taking apart, 61
ocean, 187, 190
  freezing water, 192
  hurricanes, 253
  tide pool, 146–148
opossum, 164
orchid, 159
oyster, 144

P

pangolin, 167
parrot, 168
patterns
  in lakes and ponds, 188
  in oceans, 190
  in rivers, 190
patterns (ocean water), 192
patterns, in bodies of water, 188, 190, 192
People in Science & Engineering
  Bruna, Emilio, 173–174

Eiffel, Gustave, 29–30
Ferris, John G., 197–198
Lopes, Rosaly M.C., 259–260
Tssui, Eugene, 55–56
plains, on a map, 206
plan
  architects, 67
  in design process, 8, 22
  geotechnical engineer, 275
  map making, 209
  model habitat, 149
  model tool, 129–130
plants. *See also* **flowers; trees**
  air, need for, 112
  animals depending on, 125–127
  aster, 163
  bromeliad, 160
  buffalo grass, 167
  carpet moss, 163
  climate types for, 119–120
  duckweed, 142
  erosion slowed with, 239
  ferns, 163
  in forest, 162–164
  on forest floor, 163
  grasses, 167

Index

Index